CULTURE SMART!

NICARAGUA

Russell Maddicks

·K·U·P·E·R·A·R·D·

This book is available for special discounts for bulk purchases for sales promotions or premiums. Special editions, including personalized covers, excerpts of existing books, and corporate imprints, can be created in large quantities for special needs.

For more information contact Kuperard publishers at the address below.

ISBN 978 1 85733 876 8

British Library Cataloguing in Publication Data
A CIP catalogue entry for this book is available from the British Library

First published in Great Britain
by Kuperard, an imprint of Bravo Ltd
59 Hutton Grove, London N12 8DS
Tel: +44 (0) 20 8446 2440 Fax: +44 (0) 20 8446 2441
www.culturesmart.co.uk
Inquiries: sales@kuperard.co.uk

Series Editor Geoffrey Chesler
Design Bobby Birchall

Printed in India

About the Author

RUSSELL MADDICKS is a BBC-trained journalist who has spent the last twenty years exploring the countries of Latin America and publishing his experiences in print, online, and in social media. A graduate in Economic and Social History from the University of Hull, England, he is fluent in Spanish and has worked as a regional specialist for BBC Monitoring covering political developments and regional news. Over the years he has visited Nicaragua on many extended trips. He has written for international publications, including *BBC Travel*, *National Geographic Traveller*, the *Mexico News Daily*, *Latino Life*, *ArtNews*, and *Songlines*, and is an accomplished public speaker who has given illustrated talks on Latin American destinations at book fairs, travel shows, colleges, and universities. Russell is the author of *Culture Smart! Venezuela*, *Culture Smart! Ecuador* (which won the Gold Prize at the Pearl of the Pacific International Travel Journalism Awards at FITE in 2015), *Culture Smart! Cuba* (co-author), *Culture Smart! Mexico*, and the *Bradt Guide to Venezuela*.

contents

contents

Map of Nicaragua

introduction

The largest country in Central America, Nicaragua is also one of the most diverse. A chain of hills and thick forests separates the land into two distinct areas: the surfing beaches and colonial cities of the Pacific lowlands that rise up into the northern coffee hills, inhabited by Spanish-speaking *mestizos*; and the sparsely populated Atlantic coast, which is home to Creole-speaking Afro-Caribbeans and the indigenous Miskito people who gave their name to the famed Mosquito Coast.

Nicaragua is the poorest country in the Western Hemisphere after Haiti, but Nicas, as the people are known, are proud and resilient, forged from the adversity of the country's troubled past and working hard to secure a better future. The small-town friendliness of the countryside extends to the cities, and the welcoming smiles that visitors encounter are genuine, rather than prompted by the allure of the tourist dollar.

Following the Sandinista uprising that toppled the dictator Anastasio Somoza in 1979, and the ensuing Contra War sponsored by Washington in the 1980s, the image has persisted of a country racked by conflict. There are still challenges that Nicaraguans need to work out, as the widespread protests in 2018 against the social security reforms of the Sandinista government of Daniel Ortega have proved, but travelers will find that Nicaragua is actually one of the safest countries in the Americas, and is free of the gang violence that plagues its northern neighbors.

As travelers discover the delights of this land of lakes and volcanoes, more areas are opening up to tourism, creating a market for Nicaragua's premium coffee beans, tasty chocolate made from heirloom cocoa beans, and Flor de Caña, the smoothest aged rum ever to come out of an oak barrel. Your budget will stretch further here than in other Latin American destinations, and there is a "Wow! factor" to experience around every corner, including charming colonial cities and graceful mansions, Pacific breakers producing perfect surf, high-altitude coffee plantations shrouded in clouds, world-class birdwatching in rainforest reserves, and picture-postcard Caribbean islands. There is also a chain of volcanoes along the Pacific coast that you can climb up and surf down, and volcanic crater lakes that you can swim in. You can even drive up to the lip of the Masaya volcano, just outside Managua, and stare down at the glowing red lava lake at its heart.

This small book provides readers with an insider's view of the country and its people. It explores Nicaragua's national traditions, turbulent history, tasty local dishes, fun *fiestas*, and unique cultural expressions. It arms you with key phrases in Nica-speak, or *Nicañol*, so you can break the ice when interacting with the locals, and provides insights into what the people of Nicaragua are like at home, at play, and in business, so that you really can get under the skin of this intriguing country, and make the most of your visit.

Key Facts

Offical Name	República de Nicaragua	
Population	6.08 million (2014, World Bank)	
Ethnic Makeup	69% *Mestizo* (Mixed Race); 17% White; 9% Afro-Caribbean; 5% Indigenous Amerindian (2010 census)	
Capital City	Managua	Pop. 1.1 million (2015 est.)
Main Cities	León (pop. 201,000); Masaya (166,000); Matagalpa (150,000); Chinandega (134,000); Granada (124,000); Jinotega (123,000); Estelí (122,000)	
Area	50,336 sq. miles (130,370 sq. km). Largest country in Central America	
Geography	Borders Honduras in north; Costa Rica in south; Atlantic coastline in east; Pacific in west.	
Terrain Climate	Pacific lowlands dotted with volcanoes; central highlands; Caribbean lowlands of the Mosquito Coast; freshwater Lake Nicaragua, the largest in Central America; Corn Islands in Caribbean	
Seasons	Dry season or summer (*verano*) January–June. Rainy season or winter (*invierno*) July–late November. Wettest months July–September. Sunrise about 6 a.m., sunset about 6 p.m.	Tropical. Coast dry and hot; northern highlands cooler; rainforest and Atlantic coast hot, wet, humid. Temperature year-round average daytime highs of 90°F (32°C) and lows of 75°F (23°C)
Life Expectancy	75.1 years (men 71.5; women 77.9) (2015)	
Infant Mortality	19 deaths per 1,000 live births (2015)	

Language	Official language Spanish	Creole English, Miskito, Sumo, Garifuna, Rama, also spoken
Literacy Rate	82.8% (UN 2015)	
Religion	53% Roman Catholic; 40% Evangelical Protestant	
System of Government	Democratic Republic, with a Unicameral National Assembly elected every five years. The president is chief of state and head of government, elected every five years. Country is divided into 15 Departments and 2 Autonomous Regions.	
Media	Privately owned national newspapers are *La Prensa* and *El Nuevo Diario*. Pro-Sandinista media include La Voz del Sandinismo and El19. There are hundreds of state-run and independent radio stations. Cable and satellite TV packages host international channels.	
Currency	Córdoba (C$), divided into 100 cents	
GDP Per Capita	US $4,500	
Electricity	120 volts, 60 Hz	European plugs need adaptors.
Internet Domain	.ni	
Video/TV	NTSC - DVD Zone 4	
Telephone	International dialing code 505. Cities have their own codes: Managua 2, Granada 55, León 311, Matagalpa 61, Bluefields 82, Masaya 52, Estelí 71, San Juan del Sur 4682	
Time Zone	UTC/GMT -6 hours	

LAND & PEOPLE

GEOGRAPHICAL SNAPSHOT

Nicaragua is a triangular wedge between Honduras in the north and Costa Rica to the south, with the Pacific Ocean to the west and the Caribbean to the east. The largest country in Central America, it occupies an area of 50,336 square miles (130,370 sq. km)—slightly larger than the US state of Mississippi.

The country can be divided into three broad geographical areas: the Pacific lowlands in the west, which consist of a broad and fertile plain that runs from the Golfo de Fonseca in the north to Costa Rica in the south; the central highlands, which sweep down from the forested uplands bordering Honduras through the middle of the country, effectively cutting it in half; and the Atlantic lowlands to the east, which take up almost 50 percent of the nation's territory, dominated by a long Caribbean coastline from Gracias a Dios in the north to San Juan de Nicaragua in the south, incorporating the lush Corn Islands and remote Pearl Cays.

Pacific Lowlands

You only have to glance at a topographical map of Nicaragua to see why it is known as the Land of Lakes and Volcanoes. The Pacific coast is dotted with an imposing string of twenty-five volcanoes, both active and dormant, that stretch from the huge crater lake of

Cosigüina on the Golfo de Fonseca to the twin-volcano island of Ometepe in Lago Cocibolca (Lake Nicaragua), the largest freshwater lake in Central America and the ninth-largest in the world. The lake covers an area of 3,191 square miles (8,264 sq. km) and is so vast that when the Spanish conquistadors arrived on its shores in 1523 they thought they had reached an ocean. Only when their horses started to drink from it did they realize it was a freshwater lake—and so they named it the Mar Dulce (Sweet Sea). Connected to the Caribbean Sea via the Río San Juan, Lago Cocibolca is home to bull sharks that have adapted to its low salinity, and encompasses several archipelagos, including Las Isletas, close to the colonial city of Granada, and Solentiname in the far south.

Nicaragua's other large body of fresh water, Lago Xolotlán (Lake Managua), has been cleaned up in recent years, in particular the lakeside promenade in the capital, Managua, which now has a restaurant complex named after the deposed Chilean President Salvador Allende and a pier from which pleasure boats set off on short trips.

The country's volcanoes are a huge magnet for tourists. Thrill-seekers climb to the summit of the still active Cerro Negro—the youngest volcano in Central America—and "volcano board" down the black ash slopes created by its last eruption in 1999. If you don't fancy a hike, you can drive right to the lip of the Masaya volcano, near Managua, and stare down at a bubbling lake of red-hot lava. Small belches of smoke or ash occur regularly at volcanoes like San Cristóbal, which appears on the label of Flor de Caña rum and is the tallest of Nicaragua's volcanoes at 5,725 feet (1,745 m). When Cosigüina exploded in 1835 it was the biggest eruption in Nicaragua's history, sending clouds of ash as far as Mexico and Jamaica. But even that pales in comparison to the eruption of the Mombacho volcano some 25,000 years ago, which was so explosive that rocks blown from the cone formed the 365 tiny islands of Las Isletas. As if to remind the world of the power of nature, the perfect cone of Momotombo burst dramatically back to life in 2015 after lying dormant for a hundred years.

The cause of all this volcanic action is Nicaragua's location in the Pacific Ring of Fire, a horseshoe-shaped area of seismic activity created by the juddering grind of tectonic plates that affects countries all around the Pacific rim, from New Zealand and Japan via North and Central America to Peru and Chile in South America.

Nicaragua's historic colonial cities of Granada and León are also located along the Pacific strip, and the country's top surfing beaches can be found around the tourist town of San Juan del Sur.

Central Highlands

To the east of the Pacific lowlands the cool hills around the northern cities of Matagalpa and Jinotega are Nicaragua's prime coffee country. Some of the best high-altitude Arabica shade coffee in the world is grown here on forested farms, where birdwatchers come to see the three-wattled bellbird and the resplendent quetzal in all its tail-shimmering glory. In the nineteenth century German immigrants settled here and set up coffee farms, drawn by government incentives and land grants. Their influence can still be seen today at the Selva Negra coffee hacienda, named after the Black Forest and run by descendants of those first German settlers.

Around the northern city of Estelí, the main crop is tobacco. The introduction of Cuban tobacco seeds following the Cuban revolution, and the fertility of the local soil, have led to a situation where Nicaraguan cigars regularly beat their Cuban rivals to the top spots on the annual lists of magazines like *Cigar Aficionado*. Estelí is also surrounded by national parks such as Tisey and Miraflor, where coffee cooperatives offer home-stays for foreign tourists who want to hike in the hills or learn about rural life.

Cerro Mogotón, at 6,913 feet (2,107m) Nicaragua's highest mountain, lies on the Honduran border in the Reserva Nacional Cordillera Dipilto y Jalapa in Nueva Segovia department. Also on that border is the Cañon de Somoto, a meandering canyon of deep ravines cut through some of the oldest rock formations in Central America by the Comali and Tapacali Rivers.

Atlantic Lowlands
The land along the Mosquito Coast—once the haunt of European pirates and briefly a remote outpost of the British Empire—is home to Nicaragua's last indigenous tribes, Afro-Caribbean fishing villages, and huge swathes of coastal mangroves. Covering over half the country, these sparsely populated lowlands are home to fewer than a million inhabitants.

In the north, the border with Honduras is marked by the Río Coco (or Wanky to the Miskito people)—the longest river in Central America at 466 miles (750 km) long—which flows into the Caribbean at Cabo Gracias a Dios. In the south, the Río San Juan marks the border with Costa Rica at San Juan de Nicaragua. In between, the only cities of any size are the ports of Bluefields and Bilwi (Puerto Cabezas).

Important gold reserves are mined in the jungles around the aptly named northern town of Bonanza, in an area known as the Golden Triangle, and the pristine rainforests of the Bosawas and Indio Maíz nature reserves are home to a myriad marvels of nature.

Off the coast, the palm-fringed Corn Islands are the main draw for tourists, offering lazy days on beautiful beaches and scuba diving at all levels.

CLIMATE

Due to its position north of the Equator, Nicaragua has a subtropical climate that blesses it with all-year sunshine and warm temperatures. There are two main seasons: dry and rainy. The *temporada seca* (dry season), or *verano* (summer), brings the hottest temperatures and runs from January to the end of April. It is generally dry, but short tropical downpours in the afternoon or overnight are not unusual.

The *temporada de lluvia* (rainy season), or *invierno* (winter), runs from May through to the end of the hurricane season in November. Rainfall is generally heavier in August and September, when tropical storms can bring spectacular torrential downpours, especially along the Atlantic coast and the islands of the Caribbean. Storms tend not to last long and are interspersed with bright periods of sunshine. In

December the weather can be fresh, and January is the coolest month, although fluctuations in the pattern of the rains in recent years have made it harder to predict.

It is generally hotter on the coastal lowlands, cooler in the northern uplands, and hotter, wetter, and more humid in the dense forests of the Atlantic coast.

For travelers to the Pacific lowlands, the height of the dry season can feel very hot, especially in cities like Managua and León. Granada benefits from the cooling winds coming off Lago Cocibolca, and San Juan del Sur and other Pacific beach resorts are wafted by sea breezes. An upside to the withering heat of the dry season is a reduction in flies and mosquitoes.

The benefits of traveling in the rainy season are that it doesn't rain every day, it's fresher, and the countryside is greener. Surfers also prefer the rainy months, as the rains bring heavier swells and bigger breakers.

Average temperatures in the Pacific lowlands can reach daytime highs of over 90°F (32°C) and lows of 75°F (23°C), which is a similar pattern to the Corn Islands. The highland cities of Matagalpa, Estelí, and Jinotega are always a few degrees cooler.

THE PEOPLE

Nicaragua, like its neighbors in Central America, is a *mestizo* nation—a melting pot of the indigenous Amerindian people who were here before Columbus arrived in 1502, mixed with the descendants of the Spanish conquistadors who followed in his wake and other European settlers. Some 69 percent of Nicaraguans identify as *mestizo*, and they make up the bulk of the population along the Pacific coast and in the northern highlands. The old elite of Spanish colonialists and the Europeans who got rich from coffee and the

California steamboat route in the nineteenth century make up the majority of the 17 percent identified as white, and there is also a small but well-established expat community of North Americans and Canadians in Granada, León, and San Juan del Sur.

Living along the sparsely populated Atlantic coast are most of the 9 percent of the Nicaraguan population who identify as black or Afro-Caribbean. These are descendants of Africans brought in chains to the Caribbean to work in British sugar plantations. Under the British protectorate that operated in the eighteenth century along the Mosquito Coast and out on the Corn Islands thousands of Afro-Caribbeans came to Nicaragua, mainly from Jamaica, from where the protectorate was run. Caribbean culture, music, and food are still predominant along the Mosquito Coast, and Nicaragua's Afro-Caribbeans maintain ties to their African and British past in the English Creole they speak, the *rondón* seafood soup they eat, and the maypole dances of the Tulululu *fiestas* held every May in Bluefields and elsewhere.

There are also about 500 Garifuna in the community of Orinoco, on Laguna de Perlas. Made up of African slaves who mixed with Caribs and Arawaks on the island of St. Vincent, the Garifuna were cast out from St. Vincent in 1797 by the British following slave revolts, and arrived on the shores of Roatan, in Honduras, from where they spread to Belize, Guatemala, and Nicaragua. Famous for their music and *punta* drumbeat, the Garifuna of Nicaragua keep their traditions and language alive through regular contact with other Garifuna groups in Central America.

When the Spanish first arrived in Central America they encountered a large indigenous population of Nahuatl-speakers with cultural ties to the Aztecs and Mayas of present-day Mexico, Chibcha groups from South America, and Taino groups from the Caribbean islands. Nowadays in Nicaragua, indigenous Amerindians make up only 5 percent of the population and are almost exclusively found on the Atlantic coast. The largest group is the Miskito, or Miskitu, who give their name to the Mosquito Coast. An Afro-indigenous group, the Miskito were close to the British in the eighteenth and nineteenth centuries, and their leaders were crowned kings by the English governors of Jamaica. They keep their language alive through community radio and regular festivities and cultural events in their communities. Other smaller indigenous groups, such as the Rama and the Mayagna, or Sumu, also remain on ancestral lands in the autonomous regions of the Atlantic.

Nicaraguans still refer to Arabic people—both Christian and Muslim—as *Turcos* (Turks), a legacy of the period before and after the First World War when small numbers of Lebanese Christians, Palestinians, and Syrians came to Nicaragua from the collapsing Ottoman Empire. These *Arabes*, as they are also called, can be found in Nicaragua's sprawling markets, where they are known for selling textiles and clothing at good prices.

Small Chinese communities were first established in Nicaragua in the nineteenth century on the Caribbean coast, especially in Bluefields, where they soon began trading. Moving to Managua and marrying into local families, the Chinese community spread to the main cities of the country, and *los Chinos* have a reputation for business skills. There are nowadays about 10,000 Chinese-speakers in the country. The most famous descendant of Chinese origin in Nicaragua is Arlen Siu, a celebrated martyr of the Sandinista Revolution.

Unlike its neighbors, Nicaragua does not have a large migrant population in the USA. The majority of Nicaraguans who leave looking for work head to Costa Rica, which has a floating population of anything from 400,000 to 800,000 Nicaraguans, living there legally and illegally. About 400,000 Nicaraguans live in the US, many of whom moved there in the 1980s to escape the violence of the Contra War. The main concentration is in Miami, which has a Nica population of about 150,000. The small town of Sweetwater in nearby Miami-Dade County, Florida, is even known as Little Managua as Nicaraguans make up about 16 percent of its population. Another 100,000 Nicaraguans live in California, mainly in Los Angeles and San Francisco. The Nicaraguan population in the USA has been affected by US President Donald Trump's decision to end in 2019 the Temporary Protected Status, or TPS, that was extended to Central American migrants after the devastation of Hurricane Mitch in 1998. Some fear that the end of TPS could lead to deportations of Nicaraguans at a time when remittances are so important to the economy.

A BRIEF HISTORY
The Earliest People
The long-held theory that hunter-gatherers from Siberia populated the Americas after crossing the Bering Strait at the end of the last Ice Age around 11,500 years ago has been largely revised. Evidence from the sites of Monte Verde in Chile and Serra da Capivara in Brazil suggest that early settlers may have arrived here as far back as 40,000 years ago. The first Americans didn't just walk across a land bridge from Siberia, either. Recent DNA research indicates that the Americas were

populated by different groups in several waves, and some of the early settlers probably used small boats to travel down the Pacific coast.

From the earliest times Central America has served as a bridge linking the two Americas and a melting pot of people and ideas. Ceramics and stone effigies show that over many centuries, before the arrival of Christopher Columbus, cultural influences from the Maya and Nahuatl speakers (Aztecs) of Mexico, Guatemala, and Honduras were present in Nicaragua, as were beliefs and customs brought from South America by gold-working tribes such as the Chibcha.

The oldest evidence of human habitation in Nicaragua is the Acahualinca footprints in Managua, which were left by hunter-gatherers walking along the

muddy banks of Lago de Managua some 6,000 years ago and were miraculously preserved in volcanic ash.

The Nicaraguan tribes whose names have come down to us from the chronicles of the Spanish conquest include the Nahuatl-speaking Pipil, Nicarao, Chorotega, Chontal, Lenca, Subtiaba, and Maribios along the Pacific coast, the Matagalpa in the highlands, and the ancestors of the Miskitos, Ramas, and Sumos of the Atlantic coast, who shared cultural links with South American groups.

Spanish Arrival and Conquest

Christopher Columbus became the first European to explore the Americas on his first voyage in 1492 when he "discovered" the Caribbean. The Genoan seafarer believed he had arrived in Asia, which led to the people he encountered being referred to as *Indios* (Indians), and the Caribbean islands as the West Indies. During his third voyage in 1502 to what he now called the New World he followed the Mosquito Coast and was caught in a violent storm. Finding shelter in a bay at the mouth of the Río Coco, he wrote, "*Gracias a Dios hemos salido de esas honduras*" (Thank God we have come out of those depths), thus giving names to Cabo Gracias a Dios (Cape Thank God) in Nicaragua and to the land of Honduras.

Starting out from Panama, the first expedition into the territory of present-day Nicaragua was by Gil González de Ávila, who subdued the tribe of Cacique Nicarao in 1522 but was beaten back by a fierce leader, Diriangén, in 1523 (see box opposite).

The conquistador Francisco Hernández de Córdoba had more luck in 1524, founding the towns of Granada and León and pacifying much of the Pacific coast, but his luck was short lived. In 1526 the governor

WHEN NICARAO MET THE SPANISH

When the Spanish conquistador Gil González de Ávila traveled from Panama to the Pacific coast of present-day Nicaragua in 1522 he met a local *cacique* (chief) called Nicarao, who welcomed him warmly and asked all manner of questions about Spain, the Spanish king, and the Spaniards' God. Nicarao agreed to allow his people to convert to Christianity and accept the presence of the Spanish. A rival *cacique* called Diriangén, however, saw only trouble from the foreign invaders and on April 17, 1523, engaged the Spanish in a bloody battle that lasted four hours and forced González de Ávila and his men to withdraw.

From that time on the Spanish referred to this new land as Nicaragua, which is either a combination of Nicarao with *agua* (water), because of the great lake, or means, as some historians believe, "Nicarao's tribe."

of Panama, Pedro Arias Dávila, had Hernández de Córdoba captured and beheaded as the conquistadors jostled for power and fought over the spoils of the region. A statue of Cordoba stands today by the lake in Granada, and Nicaragua's currency is named after him.

The dire consequences of the Spanish conquest for the indigenous people of Nicaragua was felt almost immediately, with war, disease, and slavery reducing an estimated population of around one million down to tens of thousands in the first thirty years.

Only in the remote forests of the highlands and the Atlantic coast did indigenous tribes stave off the yoke of Spanish conquest through fierce resistance and the natural protection afforded them by mountains and rough terrain.

With no significant gold sources to mine, or obvious natural resources to exploit, Nicaragua became one more backwater of the Spanish Empire in the Americas, a province under the jurisdiction of the Captaincy General of Guatemala.

The British Arrive

The gold, silver, and precious stones of the Incas and the rest of South America were shipped out to Spain in grand flotillas from the Colombian port of Cartagena, and the Atlantic coast of Central America, known in English as the Spanish Main, quickly became a magnet for English, French, and Dutch privateers. These pirates of the Caribbean would hide out between raids in Port Royal, Jamaica, or along the Mosquito Coast of Nicaragua. The town of Bluefields was named after the Dutch pirate Abraham Blauvelt, and it was the center of the British Protectorate that sought to establish a foothold on the Nicaraguan mainland after the Providence Island Company made the attempts at settlement of Providence Island and the Mosquito Coast in the 1630s. The English worked with the Miskito to extract dyewood and logwood from the forests of the Mosquitia region, and strong bonds were established, resulting in a curious arrangement where the Miskito chief was recognized by the British government and crowned in Jamaica. The name of the first Miskito king is lost in the annals, but his son Oldman was crowned in 1650. The last to rule the Miskito was George Augustus Frederic II, crowned in 1842, but the tradition survived after Nicaragua established control of the region until 1908. It is remembered today in the King Pulanka *fiestas*.

It was a deal between the Prussian king, the British government and the Miskito in 1849 that allowed the Moravian Church to begin the evangelization of the Mosquito Coast that continues today.

Pesky Pirates

In the seventeenth century European privateers and pirates quickly discovered that there was booty to be plundered if they followed the Rio San Juan from the Atlantic into the vast lake of Cocibolca and on to the prosperous city of Granada. The legendary pirate Sir Henry Morgan sacked the city in 1665, making off with treasure chests of silver, and the pirate Gallardillo attacked it again in 1670, leading the Spanish in 1675 to construct El Castillo de la Inmaculada Concepción (Fortress of the Immaculate Conception) to prevent the pirates from passing the Raudales del Diablo (Devil's Rapids). The fortress didn't stop the English privateer William Dampier burning down Granada in 1685, and the English came back many times. The twenty-two-year-old Horatio Nelson, hero of the Battle of Trafalgar, saw some of his first action here when he took El Castillo by force in 1780 and held it for nine months.

The Move to Independence

The collapse of Spain's empire in the Americas only came after bloody and brutal independence wars in Mexico and South America, but Central America was largely spared the bloodshed. When the Captaincy-

General of Guatemala declared its independence from Spain in September 1821, there was a brief attempt at a Mexican federation before the new republics of Guatemala, Honduras, El Salvador, Nicaragua, and Costa Rica created their own Central American Federation.

In 1838 Nicaragua broke away from the federation and declared itself an independent republic, but a simmering power struggle between the colonial capital León, which was Liberal, and prosperous Granada, which was Conservative, threatened to boil over into civil war. A compromise solution to name the village of Managua as the country's capital in 1852 only provided a brief respite from the conflict, which continued to flare up.

This was the time when the first German settlers arrived in the country, taking up government offers of land grants and setting up coffee haciendas in the northern highlands. But it was the political and business interests from the USA that were to have the biggest impact on Nicaragua.

The Age of the Steamers

The California Gold Rush that started in 1848 prompted the US railroad and shipping magnate Cornelius Vanderbilt to set up a company to transport prospective prospectors from the east coast of the USA to the west coast via Nicaragua.

Passengers from New York landed in Greytown on Nicaragua's Atlantic coast, traveled up the Rio San Juan to San Carlos, across Cocibolca (Lago de Nicaragua), and then overland to the port of San Juan del Sur for the onward trip to San Francisco.

A faster, cheaper, and safer way than traveling by stage coach across the US, Vanderbilt's Nicaragua route was an attractive alternative to an existing route through Panama and with 2,000 passengers a month it soon made a very wealthy Mr. Vanderbilt even wealthier.

William Walker and the Filibusters

In Nashville, Tennessee, where William Walker was born in 1824, there is a plaque that hails him as a "Grey-Eyed Man of Destiny." In Nicaragua he is universally reviled as the man who brought war to the country, declared himself president, tried to reintroduce slavery, and burned Granada to the ground. A talented scholar, he earned degrees in medicine and law and carved out a niche as a newspaperman before embarking on his adventures. Walker was an unlikely soldier of fortune but driven by a strong belief in Manifest Destiny—the nineteenth-century doctrine that the USA had a God-given right to spread its dominion over more primitive nations in North America—in 1852

he put together a group of filibusters (mercenaries) and invaded an area of Lower California and Sonora in Mexico. Walker's actions helped the USA to secure the Gadsden Purchase in Arizona, but the US government forced an end to his mercenary venture in Mexico and he was put on trial in California for conducting an illegal war. After defending himself ably in court, Walker walked free, but was determined to continue his filibustering. He set his eye on Nicaragua, where the civil war between the Legitimists (Conservatives) of Granada and the Democrats (Liberals) of León had flared up again. This time, Walker insisted on being invited to Nicaragua to avoid further troubles with the US legal system, and in 1855 he was duly asked by the Liberals of León to join their struggle against Granada with his small band of California mercenaries.

Following several military victories, Walker declared himself president of Nicaragua and was sworn in on July 26, 1856, in a public ceremony in the Central Plaza of Granada. His first acts as president were to reinstate slavery, declare English the official language, and offer financial inducements to encourage immigration from the southern states of the USA. Walker's rogue government was even recognized by US President Franklin Pierce.

Nevertheless, his luck didn't last long enough for his vision of a Nicaragua run by slave-owning Southern whites to take shape. The first major defeat of his mercenary army was at the Battle of San Jacinto on September 14, 1856. The outnumbered Nicaraguan forces were victorious after Andrés Castro, who had run out of bullets, dropped his gun and furiously began throwing stones at the filibusters, taking one down and spurring on his compatriots. Castro survived the battle and found fame as a national hero. His brave actions on that day are celebrated across Nicaragua every year on September 14.

Finally, on December 18, 1856, with Granada surrounded by 4,000 Central American troops who had come to oust him, William Walker showed his true colors and fled the city.

His parting gift to the people of Nicaragua was to order his soldiers to burn Granada to the ground, to instil, as he put it, "a salutary dread of American justice." After two weeks of fire and fury, all that remained of historic Granada were the inscriptions that Walker's men had left on the ruins: *Aqui Fue Granada*—Here Was Granada.

In 1857 Walker was sent by the US Navy back to New York, where he wrote about his exploits in a book entitled *The War in Nicaragua*. He did not escape justice, however. In 1860, he returned to Central America on a final filibustering expedition, but was caught by the British Navy and handed over to the Honduran authorities. On September 12, 1860, the thirty-six-year-old Walker was shot by a firing squad. He is buried in Trujillo, Honduras, in a simple grave.

Enter the Marines

The 1860s saw the end of the British claim over the Mosquito Coast, which was gradually incorporated into Nicaragua under President José Santos Zelaya in an attempt to unify the country. However, Zelaya's supression of a conservative military uprising in 1909, in which two US citizens were killed, led to the arrival of US warships and the beginning of a long period of US intervention in Nicaraguan affairs. US interest in Central America had been fueled at this time by the inter-oceanic canal being built in Panama, and there was talk in the US Congress of backing a canal through Nicaragua instead.

Continued unrest in the country led embattled President Adolfo Díaz to turn to the USA for help, and US Marines were soon involved in the conflict, operating on Nicaraguan soil from 1912 to 1933. In the meantime, the Bryan–Chamorro Treaty was signed with the US government in 1914, which gave it control "in perpetuity" over any inter-oceanic canal that might be built in the country, effectively protecting its interests in the Panama Canal.

From Sandino to the Somozas

With his trademark hat and lace-up boots, General Augusto Calderón Sandino (1895–1934), is the country's most iconic national hero. The illegitimate son of a hacienda owner and fervent nationalist, General Sandino

led a small rebel army from 1927 that was dedicated to driving the US Marines from his homeland and tearing up the Bryan–Chamorro Treaty. The US government dismissed him at the time as a bandit, but against all the odds his military campaigns were successful and the Marines shipped out in 1933. The peace was far harder to win than the war. The USA had trained a local force known as the National Guard, which was led by Anastasio Somoza García (1896–1956), who was known to his enemies as "Tacho." On February 23, 1934, Sandino came to Managua to sign a peace deal with President Juan Bautista Sacasa, but was ambushed by members of the National Guard and executed. His body was never found.

General Somoza, meanwhile, went on to establish a cruel family dictatorship that with US support was able to run Nicaragua as if it were their own private hacienda for more than forty years while they amassed huge personal wealth. Tacho Somoza was eventually shot dead in 1956 in the city of León by the poet Rigoberto López Pérez. His son and successor Luis Anastasio Somoza Debayle (1922–67) died of a heart attack.

In the end it took a popular uprising led by the Sandinistas—a group named in honor of Sandino—to force the last Somoza to flee. On July 17, 1979, Anastasio Somoza Debayle, or "Tachito," flew out of Managua for Miami. US President Jimmy Carter refused him entry, but he was offered exile in Paraguay by the dictator Alfredo Stroessner. The plane was allegedly filled with cash and bullion, part of the US$2 billion fortune the Somozas are estimated to have pocketed while in power. His exile in Asunción was short-lived; in September 1980 a Sandinista commando unit blew up his car with a rocket-propelled grenade.

The Sandinista Revolution

An inspiration across Latin America and the world, the Sandinista Revolution was a popular uprising against the Somoza regime led by the Frente Sandinista de Liberación Nacional (FSLN), or Sandinista National Liberation Front. Founded in 1961 by Carlos Fonseca, Silvio Mayorga, and Tomás Borge, the Sandinistas were just one of a handful of the revolutionary student groups that emerged from the universities of León and Managua in the 1960s.

With close ties to Cuba, which offered military training to the young fighters, the Sandinistas were able to mount an effective campaign against the National Guard, helped by the popular dissatisfaction with the Somoza dictatorship that saw protest marches and national strikes bring the country to a standstill.

A turning point for many Nicaraguans was the cynical government response to the devastating earthquake that struck Managua on December 23, 1972, killing some 10,000 people, injuring another 20,000, and leaving more than 300,000 homeless. Instead of distributing the foreign aid supplies and financial donations that flooded in following the disaster, the Somoza regime and its cronies were seen to be profiting from the tragedy and doing little to assist survivors. Reconstruction only began in earnest in the 1990s.

Another key moment in the revolution was the assassination on January 10, 1978, of Pedro Joaquín Chamorro, the editor of opposition newspaper *La Prensa*, who was shot eighteen times by gunmen who drew up alongside his car in Managua. Widespread protests throughout the country followed the shooting and led to open fighting against the National Guard by Sandinista rebels, who dressed in olive-green fatigues like the Cuban revolutionaries who had inspired them.

In Managua on August 22, 1978, the Sandinistas pulled off a daring attack on the National Palace while the assembly was in session. Led by Eden Pastora, the small group of Sandinistas took 2,000 hostages and received a large ransom and the release of imprisoned Sandinistas in return for the kidnapped assembly members.

As the towns and cities fell like dominoes to the FSLN in June 1979 it became clear that the days of the Somoza dictatorship were numbered. But when the final victory came on July 17, 1979, and the Sandinistas entered Managua for victory celebrations in front of the earthquake-damaged cathedral, they had to deal with a country that had been bankrupted by the civil strife, a treasury that had been plundered by the Somoza regime, and a capital still in ruins.

The Contra War

US President Jimmy Carter sent aid to help rebuild Nicaragua's shattered economy in the early days of the post-Somoza government, but the Sandinistas' close relationship with Cuba and Russia, their Marxist-Leninist leanings, and their land redistribution policies led to conflict with Ronald Reagan's administration. The result was US backing for the Contrarrevoluciónarios, or Contras, made up at the start by former National Guard members who attacked Nicaragua from bases in Honduras. In the autonomous regions of the Atlantic coast, indigenous groups like the Miskito were also fighting for greater

control over their territory. The Sandinistas led highly praised literacy campaigns that were supported by foreign *Brigadistas* from the US and Europe, but as the 1980s wore on the increasingly bloody Contra war took a huge toll on the ailing economy and claimed some 30,000 lives. The Iran-Contra arms for cash scandal exposed the covert methods the Reagan administration was using to finance the Contra War, which was only one element of the concerted US attempts to isolate and topple the Sandinista government. In the end, exhausted by the war, both sides agreed to peace talks, which resulted in the 1990 election in which Violeta Chamorro, the widow of the slain newspaperman Pedro Joaquín Chamorro, led an umbrella group of Liberal and right-wing parties to victory over the Sandinista candidate, Daniel Ortega.

Nicaragua Since 1990

The pendulum swing of politics from the radical leftist leanings of the socialist Sandinistas to the pro-business government of Violeta Chamorro did not result in any great gains for the average Nicaraguan. An IMF-sponsored austerity and privatization program included cuts to welfare services and the sale of the railway and other state-owned assets at rock-bottom prices. The Constitutional Liberal Party (PLC) governments of Arnoldo Alemán in 1996 and Enrique Bolaños in 2001 were similarly slow to bring economic progress to the country and were widely criticized for corruption, and Alemán was convicted of embezzlement in 2003.

Nicaragua was one of the beneficiaries of the debt relief inspired by the "Live 8" rock concerts in 2005 that shed light on the plight of the world's poorest nations and led to much of Nicaragua's foreign debt's being written off by international lending agencies.

Long-time candidate Daniel Ortega brought the Sandinistas back into power in 2006 with a softer campaign that saw the red and black of the Sandinista flag replaced by pinks and purples, and slogans that declared the Sandinistas were "Christian, Socialist, and In Solidarity." The new approach was devised by

Rosario Murillo, Ortega's wife; it was successful again in 2011, and in the couple's landslide victory in 2016, when she ran as vice-president.

Ten years of "Danielismo" saw all the economic indices spike upward as peace, political stability, low crime rates, and cozy relations between the government, the business sector, and the Catholic Church all combined to attract investment and boost tourism.

The announcement that the government was studying a US $50-billion project to build an inter-oceanic canal with a Chinese investor raised a few eyebrows and prompted environmental groups and indigenous communities on the proposed route of the canal to protest. In the end, losses incurred on the Chinese stock market saw the canal project shelved, but the questions raised about the Ortega-Murillo government continued.

In 2018, protests by pensioners over plans to raise pension contributions and lower payouts led to ugly clashes with so-called Sandinista *turbas* (gangs), which sparked a national outcry against the government and calls for change from young student activists.

Subsequent protests that saw barricades being manned in cities and towns across the country laid bare the deep divisions that still exist in Nicaraguan society, even within the Sandinista party.

The future that Nicaragua deserves—the prosperous, progressive Nicaragua that Nicaraguans desire—depends on how well these rifts can be healed and on who emerges to replace Daniel Ortega.

GOVERNMENT

Nicaragua is a democratic republic, with a president elected by universal suffrage every five years who is both the head of state and the head of government and has the power to appoint the vice-president and a cabinet of ministers. Originally the president was limited to one term, but in 2009 the Supreme Court overturned the ban on consecutive terms, allowing President Daniel Ortega of the Sandinista Front to run again, successfully. In 2014, the Sandinista-controlled National Assembly voted to scrap term limits altogether, and President Ortega was able to win a third consecutive term, with First Lady Rosario Murillo as his vice president.

The legislative branch consists of a unicameral Asamblea Nacional (National Assembly) of ninety-two deputies who are elected every five years at the same time as presidential elections. Proportional representation and party lists are used to elect ninety of the deputies, twenty of whom are elected nationally, and seventy who represent the country's fifteen departments and two autonomous regions. The last two seats are given to the outgoing president (or vice-president if the president is reelected) and the runner-up in the most recent presidential election.

The National Assembly appoints the sixteen judges who sit on the Supreme Court in Managua, which is the highest court in the land and has the power to make changes to the constitution, and the seven magistrates of the Supreme Electoral Council (CSE), which oversees elections.

The country is divided into fifteen departments: Boaco, Carazo, Chinandega, Chontales, Estelí, Granada, Jinotega, León, Madriz, Managua, Masaya, Matagalpa, Nueva Segovia, Rivas, and Río San Juan. There are also two autonomous regions: the North Caribbean Coast Autonomous Region (RACCN), and the South Caribbean Coast Autonomous Region (RACCS).

The departments and autonomous regions are divided into 153 Alcaldías Municipales (municipalities) run by an *alcalde* (mayor) and a municipal council (*concejo municipal*), elected by popular vote.

THE ECONOMY

Something of a sleepy backwater in Spanish colonial times, and with no fossil fuels to exploit, Nicaragua's economy has relied for centuries on exports of beef, coffee, and gold. Today it is the second-poorest country in the Western Hemisphere, after Haiti. Some 45 percent of the population still live in the countryside, where work is often seasonal, families are large, and household incomes are lower.

Following the Sandinista Revolution, the drawn-out and devastating Contra War, and a series of natural disasters that set back progress, the Nicaraguan economy started to improve markedly from 2010, although a long period of protests and uncertainty in 2018 created a serious slowdown in economic growth.

After the Sandinistas returned to power in 2007, the country saw ten years of stability and an opening to private enterprise that helped the economy grow by roughly 5 percent a year between 2012 and 2017, outstripping most countries in Latin America.

Low wages, tax incentives, an increase in local purchasing power, and the benefits of Nicaragua's membership in the Central American–Dominican Republic Free Trade Agreement (CAFTA–DR), all encouraged foreign firms from North America, Europe, and Asia to set up shop in the country.

The government also created more than forty Free Trade Zones—industrial parks located near ports and major cities where factories turn out textiles, clothes, and cigars, and prepare bananas for export. The Free Trade Zone regime has become the most dynamic sector of the national economy and has been expanded to encompass call centers and technology companies.

The sectors that have most benefited from foreign investment include tourism, telecommunications, the service industry, mining, and renewable energy initiatives such as wind turbines and geothermal power generated from the country's numerous active volcanoes. Nicaragua's home-grown staples have also seen a boom. The excellent quality of the country's coffee, cocoa beans, tobacco, bananas, beef, and shrimp are now recognized around the world, and have attracted growing interest from foreign entrepreneurs in the USA, Europe, Asia, and elsewhere in Latin America.

Despite a sometimes rocky political relationship with the US government over the last few years, Nicaragua has actively encouraged US companies to operate here. The country's most widely dispersed supermarket chain, Palí—and the hypermarket Maxi-

Palí stores—are run by the US firm Walmart, which also runs the upscale supermarket chain La Unión and has now opened two large outlets in Managua under its own name. Franchised US food chains, including McDonald's, Pizza Hut, Papa John's, Subway, and Hooters, can be found in shiny modern malls in Managua, and are artfully tucked away—so as not to spoil the aesthetic—in historic buildings in colonial cities such as Granada and León.

Another important element to Nicaragua's business landscape is the expat community—the large numbers of US, Canadian, and European nationals who have relocated to tourism hotspots like Granada, San Juan del Sur, León, Estelí, Matagalpa, and the Corn Islands. Hotels, resorts, surf schools, yoga camps, restaurants, bars, micro-breweries, and real estate ventures run by expats have played a significant part in Nicaragua's tourism boom, and have brought in new business models and a greater diversification of tourism-related products and services to the country.

VALUES & ATTITUDES

It's hard to generalize about Nicaraguans. As we have seen, the country is divided along religious lines between Catholics and Protestants, along class lines between a small number of haves, many have-nots, and a growing number of in-betweens, and along cultural lines between Spanish-speakers on the Pacific coast and Creole- and Miskito-speakers in the Atlantic and Caribbean islands. But, despite these differences, Nicaraguans are fairly united when it comes to their values and attitudes, their pride in their country, their loyalty to the family, their love of the local food you can get at a *fritanga* (street-side barbecue), their determination not to miss a *fiesta*, and their struggle to achieve a better future for their children.

FAMILY VALUES

In a country where living and working with parents and other relatives is the norm rather than the exception, it is no surprise that the family is precious to Nicaraguans. This is where people's first loyalties lie, especially when an emergency arises, or money or some other support is needed. In cities, towns, and rural communities you will find grandparents, parents, and children living together. It is also typical for brothers, sisters, aunts, uncles, cousins, and godparents to live in close proximity. A round of family occasions such as christenings, birthday parties, marriages, and funerals, and celebrations such as Christmas and New Year, also helps to strengthen family bonds. And when it comes

to vacations, many Nicaraguan families prefer to be together, with three generations going to the beach, or visiting relations in other parts of the country.

CHILDREN

Nicaragua is a country of young people—more than 35 percent are below the age of fifteen. It also has the highest teenage pregnancy rates in Latin America. Some 28 percent of women give birth before they are eighteen, many of them below the legal age of consent, which is sixteen. This is partly due to ignorance about sex and contraception, and partly because they follow the pattern set by other girls in their family. Some parents might be angry when faced with a pregnant teenage daughter, but most extended families will help them and take on some of the parenting duties. Children are generally seen as bringing joy to the family, and are doted on. On the flip side, as they grow older they may also be called upon to work alongside their parents to boost the family's finances.

The result is that everywhere you go in Nicaragua you'll see children. At the market they are sitting with their mothers as they sell fish or fruit, and in the forest they help their fathers gather firewood. Children are included in the everyday lives of their parents and grandparents to a greater extent than they would be in the USA or Europe.

THE ELDERLY

From a very young age, Nicaraguans are taught to respect their elders. A younger person may address an older, non-family member as *Madre* (mother) or *Padre* (father), or use a deferential term like *Don* or *Doña*. The elderly couple who run the local *pulpería* (corner shop) will be known as Doña Josefina and Don Ramon, for example.

For most Nicaraguans the concepts of living in a nuclear family, having parties without inviting all your relatives, or putting your elderly parents in a residential care home seem strange. It is typical for grandparents or elderly relatives to remain in the family house or be cared for by younger relatives.

This is true for rich and poor alike. As a result, many elderly relatives play an important part in looking after children while parents are at work, which forms bonds across the generations.

NATIONAL PRIDE

Nicaraguans are intensely proud of the country's two national heroes: the poet Rubén Darío, whose writings sparked a literary revolution across Latin America, and General Augusto C. Sandino, a rebel who successfully fought against US occupation in the 1930s and inspired the Sandinista Revolution. If there's a third place, it has to go to the champion boxer Alexis Argüello.

Nicaraguans are also fiercely proud of their blue and white flag, the coat of arms it carries, their traditional dishes like *nacatamales*, *vigoron*, and *vaho*, their magnificent lakes and volcanoes, and anything else that sets them apart from their Central American neighbors.

ATTITUDES TOWARD RELIGION

Roman Catholicism may be on the wane owing to the rise of Protestant and Evangelical Churches, but in the not so distant past more than 80 percent of the population were practicing Catholics or at least raised in the Catholic faith. Brought to Nicaragua by the Spanish priests who accompanied the sixteenth-century Conquistadors, the Catholic religion offered a way of imposing a unified set of beliefs across an ethnically and linguistically divided region, and helped the Spanish to rule their new Latin American colonies. It also helped to

foster and maintain conservative attitudes toward sex, marriage, divorce, abortion, and homosexuality that are only slowly starting to change.

The influence of Catholicism can be seen today in the large attendances at Sunday services and the huge turnouts for festivals and *fiestas* in honor of patron saints. If you want to see Nicaraguans join together in celebration of a Catholic icon, you need only attend the uniquely Nicaraguan Gritería celebrations in honor of the Virgin Mary on December 7, when food, fireworks, and songs bring the whole country out on to the streets. Even those who don't go to church might place a candle in front of a Catholic saint and say a prayer in time of need or when a relative is sick. Baptisms, first communions, confirmations, weddings, and funerals are still important milestones in people's lives.

The number of Protestant religious groups has mushroomed in the last forty years, driven in part by the work of missionary groups such as Southern Baptists, the Church of Jesus Christ of Latter-Day Saints (Mormons), and Jehovah's Witnesses. There are hundreds of such Churches, and they minister to about 40 percent of the population.

LOVE AND MARRIAGE

With extended families living in cramped accommodation, bringing home a *jaño* (boyfriend) or *jaña* (girlfriend) to spend the night is generally not allowed, so young lovers are restricted to park-bench smooching or a stolen hour in a love hotel if they can afford it. However, teenage pregnancy statistics make it clear that, despite the strictures of both Catholic and Protestant Churches, sex is happening outside marriage in Nicaragua. Among the less well off, it's typical to find single mothers living at home with the folks, or unmarried couples who have had a child together living with parents until they can afford to marry. Men from wealthy families might wait until they are in a financial position to start a home of their own.

A generation ago, many Nicaraguans came from very large families, with up to seven children being common in rural areas and ten not being overly unusual. Nowadays, with greater access to sex education and contraception, the average family size has come down to two or three children per couple, although poor rural and indigenous families still tend to have more children than rich urban ones.

Divorce is legal in Nicaragua, and in general there is no social stigma attached to it, except within some strict religious groups.

Abortion

The Catholic Church's strong opposition to abortion has meant that it is illegal in all circumstances, even where the mother's life is in danger and in cases of rape. Sanctions are harsh, with a one-to-four-year prison sentence for a woman who has had an abortion, and a three-to-six-year prison sentence for the person who performs it. This has led some women who want a termination to put their lives at risk by turning to back-street abortionists. No change to the law is expected under the current Sandinista government, which has focused its efforts on providing better prenatal care at *casas maternas*—midwife-staffed houses where mothers-to-be can get dietary assistance, health care, and a place to rest in the days leading up to the birth.

PRIDE, HONOR, AND *MACHISMO*

In the sense that Nicaraguan women do virtually all the cooking, cleaning, and child rearing and have to earn a living as well, you could classify Nicaragua as a "macho" country. Of course *machismo* is not unique to Nicaragua. The stereotypical Latin American man is strong, decisive, and stoic, unafraid of danger, and quick to defend any slight against his family or country. This is a man who is dynamite in the bedroom and deliberately useless in the kitchen. He's a man's man, who can hold his drink and heroically wrestle a bull to the ground if needed—but he can also be demanding and take romantic rejection badly. Times are slowly changing, and there is a concerted campaign to clamp down on the negative aspects of macho behavior, especially toward wives and partners, but even now you'll rarely find a Nicaraguan man doing the daily cooking.

You still hear *piropos* (poetic or not-so-poetic compliments) spoken as women walk by, and some at least try to be funny; but overtly sexual *piropos*—like wolf whistles—come close to harassment. Anybody who is targeted in the street by a hissed *tss-tss-tss* or an attempt at a *piropo* should do as Nicaraguan women do: ignore it, and keep walking.

Nicaraguan women, in turn, should not be underestimated. Strong, determined, and capable, they have achieved the kind of gender equality in education and government that led to Nicaragua's taking tenth place in the World Economic Forum's ranking of top countries for female equality.

HOMOSEXUALITY IN A MACHO SOCIETY

A prevailing macho culture, bolstered by traditional Catholic and more recent Evangelical views on the roles played by men and women in society, has meant that the LGBTI community in Nicaragua has struggled to gain full equality under the law. Although there was a more liberal attitude to sex under the Sandinista government that took power after the fall of the Somoza dictatorship, homosexuality was effectively criminalized in 1992 by new laws passed under President Violeta Chamorro.

It wasn't until 2008 that homosexuality was finally legalized and the age of consent set at sixteen for both heterosexuals and homosexuals. Laws against discrimination in the workplace based on sexual orientation have been enacted, but same-sex partners cannot marry legally in Nicaragua, and cannot adopt children under the revised Family Code of 2015.

In general, however, Nicaraguan society is becoming more tolerant in its attitudes to sexual diversity. An annual Gay Pride festival that was first held on June 28, 1991, in Managua, to commemorate the Stonewall riots for gay rights in New York, is now also celebrated in Granada, León, Matagalpa, and other towns. There is also an annual Miss Gay Nicaragua pageant, held in early June, which aims to promote a greater tolerance of sexual diversity and tackle homophobia. These public events are well attended, raise awareness of LGBTI issues, and get positive coverage in the local news. In general, however, the LGBTI scene is quite discreet, and overt displays of affection are rarely seen.

ATTITUDES TOWARD FOREIGNERS

Most Nicaraguans canot afford to travel outside their own country, and their experience of foreign countries is limited to what they learn at school and see in the media and movies. The exceptions are the well-traveled jet-setters from the wealthy elite, students sponsored to study abroad, church members funded by mission groups, and economic migrants who have worked in neighboring Costa Rica or the USA.

Nicaraguans are genuinely interested in meeting foreign visitors and will try out their English to find out more about you. Sports are great conversation starters, and generally lead to questions about your opinions of Nicaragua. Show respect for Nicaragua and its culture, and demonstrate that you have bothered to learn a few words of the lingo, and Nicaraguans will respond with the warmth and hospitality for which they are famous. Keep conversations light, stick to positive impressions, and you may even make some firm friends. Pick holes in the place, and the response won't be so welcoming.

Don't Go Home, Gringo!

It seems counterintuitive, but despite the armed occupation of the country by US Marines in the 1930s, the official US support for the brutal Somoza dictatorship, Ronald Reagan's backing for the costly and destructive Contra War, and the more recent actions against the country by the US government, like the 2017 Nica Act, visitors from the USA can expect a warm and friendly reception in Nicaragua.

Drawn by the good weather, cheaper cost of living, and ease of integrating, thousands of retired US citizens have set up home in expat havens such as Granada, San Juan del Sur, and the coffee hills around Matagalpa and Jinotega. Many US citizens have started tourism businesses. Others are involved in solidarity projects, building schools, supporting cooperatives, and volunteering. People might not agree with the way the USA wields its power, and Donald Trump would undoubtedly be booed if he were ever to visit, but people genuinely like and appreciate the fact that US tourists, expats, and volunteers are eager to visit their country.

National pride comes into it, and not being bullied or treated like a second-class citizen by a more powerful neighbor. Nicaraguans want to enjoy the benefits of US culture when it comes to watching movies and shopping the US chains you find in Nicaragua, but they are also fiercely proud of their own traditions.

ATTITUDE TOWARD "TICOS"

With a border dispute over the Río San Juan that has rumbled on for decades, and spats over who has the right to call *gallo pinto* their national dish, it is no wonder that Nicaraguans and Costa Ricans have a relationship that is sometimes frosty. Nicaraguans maintain that Costa Rica "stole" the area of Guanacaste in 1825, while Costa Ricans complain that immigrant Nicas work illegally in their country and commit crimes there. Nicas counter that the Costa Rican economy would crumble without the low-paid work they do as nannies, cleaners, and construction workers, and that getting work permits is unnecessarily complicated. Every now and then an incident will set off an avalanche of recriminations and tit-for-tat diplomatic reactions, but seldom do problems escalate beyond words or the temporary tightening of border regulations.

Costa Rica's relative prosperity has made it a powerful magnet for Nicaraguans seeking a higher income to save up for a better life back home. Stories of Nicaraguan migrants being mistreated or exploited have fostered a perception in Nicaragua that Ticos (Costa Ricans) look down on their northern neighbors. However, ordinary Ticos and Nicas get on well and Costa Ricans represent a growing percentage of tourist arrivals in Nicaragua.

NICARAGUAN HUMOR
Nicaraguans love to laugh. Life can be tough but people get by as best they can, and often it's the ones with the toughest circumstances who'll give you the biggest smile as you walk past. You don't hear much in the way of irony and sarcasm; humor tends to be earthy and direct, based on clever wordplay, puns, and double meanings that often have a sexual connotation.

Because they grow up in big families and forge lifelong friendships with close neighbors and schoolmates, they are used to the gentle joshing and banter that comes with close-knit groups, and will often give each other funny nicknames. The closer the friendship, the crueler the nicknames tend to be, but getting a nickname is quite an honor, because it makes you one of the gang, part of the group.

People find comedy in most situations, and are quick to mock, but they are also proud and can be sensitive. Make fun of them, or anything they hold dear, and they won't be amused. Joking about the Nicaraguan soccer team's world ranking won't win you any new friends. Jokes about somebody's family are inadvisable, while disrespecting someone's mother will be met with an invitation: "Step outside."

WORK ETHIC AND TIMEKEEPING
Nicaraguans are hardworking and still live by the "rise with the sun, sleep when it sets" philosophy you find in

rural communities all over the world. They will also take their own time to get things done, as the intense heat of the day makes rushing around counterproductive. This can give clock-punching Gringos the impression that Nicaraguans are slow, when in fact they are just working to a different rhythm. If you want to get anything done in Nicaragua you have to adjust to Nica Time and leave plenty of wriggle room through the day to deal with the unexpected, such as traffic delays, tropical rains, electricity outages, or a local fiesta.

CLASS, RACE, AND ETHNIC MINORITIES

Nicaraguans fought a revolution to topple a dictator, and the post-revolution Sandinista government of the 1980s experimented with many progressive policies to try to establish a fairer society and eradicate class differences. Under Spanish rule there was a strict social hierarchy that started with the Spanish-born administrators at the top and continued down on the basis of color and race. This oligarchy of rich white families ruling over *mestizos*, African slaves, and indigenous people changed little over the centuries and created an ingrained racism that has been very hard to shift. In Nicaragua, there is still a rich elite encompassing a few families, some of them Sandinistas, a small—but growing—middle class, and then the majority of people working hard to make ends meet.

The country is also divided geographically into the Spanish-speaking Pacific strip and highlands, which are mainly *mestizo*, and the less economically developed English-Creole speaking Atlantic coast, which is predominantly Afro-Nicaraguan and indigenous. While you do encounter some racist attitudes, the Sandinista revolution did much to foster a more accepting society.

chapter three

CUSTOMS &
TRADITIONS

Following the conquest of Nicaragua's indigenous tribes led by Gil González de Ávila, Francisco Hernández de Córdoba, and other gold-greedy conquistadors, evangelizing Spanish priests came to impose the Catholic faith on the Nicarao, Chorotega, Sutiava, and Matagalpa peoples they encountered. To aid the conversion of their new flocks, the priests cleverly incorporated local rituals and beliefs into Church ceremonies and *fiestas*, beginning a process of *mestizaje* (mixing) that has profoundly shaped Nicaraguan society and culture. This is reflected in the annual festival calendar, which combines the movable feasts of the Catholic Church with unique elements taken from indigenous traditions. The calendar also reflects the country's more recent history, with the celebration of important dates, such as the declaration of Central American Independence in 1821, the battles that led to the defeat of the US filibuster William Walker in the 1850s, and the Sandinista Revolution that toppled the dictatorship of Anastasio Somoza in 1979.

Along the Atlantic coast the brief period of British control has left a distinct legacy, marked by the use of English Creole, maypole dancing, and Afro-Caribbean and Garifuna traditions that share cultural ties with the wider Caribbean.

Ancient customs and beliefs are also preserved in Nicaragua's many masked dance festivals, and in the spooky ghost stories of the colonial period along with the ghoulish characters they introduced to popular culture. The myths and legends of the Miskitu and Rama indigenous groups, meanwhile, give us a glimpse of life before the coming of the Spanish, when people lived more closely attuned to nature.

FESTIVALS AND HOLIDAYS

There's a holiday, *fiesta*, or saint's day celebrated somewhere in Nicaragua on nearly every day of the year. Sometimes it feels as if *días feriados* (public holidays) and *fiestas* (feast days, or festivals) are running into each other to make one long holiday, especially in Masaya and in the surrounding white-painted villages (Pueblos Blancos). The *fiesta* in honor of San Jeronimo, the patron saint of Masaya, is the longest in Latin America, lasting eighty days. Other celebrations end only when the *chicheros* (brass bands) are too tired— or too drunk—to play on.

March through June can also seem like an endless round of parties, as movable feasts like Semana Santa

(HolyWeek/Easter), Corpus Christi, and Carnaval merge into a blur of religious processions, parades of ox carts, street parties, marching bands, baton-twirling majorettes, and fireworks. Many of these local *fiestas* feature *hípicas* (horse parades), with local beauty queens riding through town alongside Stetson-wearing *vaqueros* (cowboys), and horses trained to dance to the carnival music of the *chicheros*. Very often these *hípicas* are followed by rodeos, with bull riding, and even fights between local boys armed with bull penises stretched and cured to form leathery swords.

If you plan to travel to any of the major festivals, or to follow the crowds to the beach, booking transport and accommodation well in advance is essential, and you should expect bus and plane terminals to be hectic. Disruptions to the transport system at these times can leave you stranded in the more remote locations, so be prepared for delays.

It is typical for businesses to shut down completely on public holidays, including government offices, banks, shops, and restaurants, which can be frustrating for tourists on a tight schedule. When a public holiday falls on a Thursday or a Tuesday, many people will take the Friday or the Monday as an extra day off, which is known as making a *puente* (bridge), so that they can enjoy a four-day weekend.

PUBLIC HOLIDAYS

January 1: Año Nuevo (New Year's Day)
March/April: Jueves Santo (Holy Thursday); Viernes Santo (Good Friday)
May 1: Día del Trabajador (Labor Day)
July 19: Día de la Revolución Popular Sandinista (Sandinista Popular Revolution Anniversary)
September 14: Batalla de San Jacinto (Battle of San Jacinto)
September 15: Independencia de Centroamérica (Central American Independence Day)
December 8: Inmaculada Concepción de Maria (Immaculate Conception of the Virgin Mary)
December 25: Navidad (Christmas Day)

Año Viejo (New Year's Eve: 31 December)
Nicaraguans like to greet *el año nuovo* (the new year) with a big party that also says good-bye to *el año viejo* (the old year). Families gather together at home to enjoy a large meal, which is eaten late, between 9:00 p.m. and midnight. Turkey is gaining popularity, but traditionally Nicaraguans will prepare the same foods as they eat for Christmas dinner: *nacatamales*, *arroz a la Valenciana* (a fancy rice dish), roast pork, suckling pig, and *relleno navideño* (a stuffing made of meat, capers, olives, currants, and nuts). New Year's Eve parties are generally lively events, with dancing to festive music such as cumbias, *norteñas*, reggaeton, and the Latin pop hits of the day.

Many Nicaraguans wear new clothes to start the year looking good, but there are lots of beliefs about how to attract luck. Those looking for love wear red underwear. Some people put $50 in their right shoe to bring prosperity. Many eat twelve grapes in the time it takes to strike the twelve chimes of midnight to bring luck in the following year. Others take a suitcase and run around the block to ensure a year of happy travels.

One tradition aimed at starting the New Year fresh and getting rid of the problems of the past is to sweep out the house on the stroke of midnight. A more dramatic—and more deafening—tradition is to make a life-size cloth and papier-mâché effigy of a *viejo* (old man) or *vieja* (old woman) and burn it, in a ritual known as *la quema del año viejo* (the burning of the old year). Some people write out a list of bad things that have happened over the past year and slip it into the clothes of the effigy before it is burned. Typically holding a cigarette or cigar in one hand and a bottle of *guaro* (cane alcohol; moonshine) in the other to represent the vices of the bad old year, the effigies are packed with gunpowder and fireworks to ensure that the symbolic burning goes off with a bang when they are dragged out into the street and set alight.

King Pulanka (January, February)

The largest indigenous group on the Atlantic coast is the Miskito. Their most important cultural festival is the King Pulanka, a celebration of cultural pride that typically starts in the village of Tuapi in January and is then held in other communities around Bilwi (Puerto Cabezas). The election of a king and queen harks back to the days when the British had direct links with the rulers of the Mosquito Coast, such as King Oldman, who was taken in the 1640s to visit King Charles I, and King Jeremy I, who was crowned in Jamaica in the 1650s. The party ended for the Miskito rulers in

1894, when King Robert Henry Clarence was deposed and Mosquitia was incorporated into Nicaragua by President Jose Santos Zelaya, but King Pulanka revives the memories of past Miskito glories. Nowadays, Miskito, English Creole, and Spanish are all part of the cultural mix in the villages along the coast, and traditional music swings to a lively Caribbean beat.

International Poetry Festival (February)
Nicaragua is known as a nation of poets and is the birthplace of Rubén Darío, one of Latin America's most important literary figures—so what better place to hold one of the most prestigious literary events in the poetic calendar? For a whole week the historic streets and plazas of the colonial city of Granada are given over to hundreds of poets from three dozen countries, who wax lyrical to an audience of enthralled locals and literary types who flock here from around the world to enjoy this homage to the spoken word.

OTHER HOLIDAYS AND FESTIVALS

January 6: Día de los Reyes (Epiphany)
February: Festival Internacional de Poesía de Granada (Granada International Poetry Festival)
February/March: Carnaval (Carnival)
May: Maypole dancing in Bluefields
May 30: Día de la Madre (Mother's Day)
June 23: Día del Padre (Father's Day)
June 24: San Juan Bautista (St. John the Baptist)
August 27-29: Crab Soup Festival on Corn Island
October 12: Día de la Resistencia Indígena, Negra, y Popular (Indigenous, Black, and Popular Resistance Day)
December 24: Nochebuena (Christmas Eve)
December 28: Día de Los Inocentes (Feast of the Holy Innocents)

The Blessing of the Dogs in Honor of San Lázaro

One of Nicaragua's most colorful traditions takes place on the Sunday before the beginning of Semana Santa (Holy Week), when dog owners dress their pets in costumes and take them to the Santa María Magdalena Church in Monimbó, a neighborhood of Masaya, to be blessed by a priest in a special Mass. The event has become so famous that it attracts dog lovers from all over Nicaragua, and INTUR, the Nicaraguan Tourism Board, holds a contest and gives prizes for the dog in the best costume.

Semana Santa (March/April)

In this strongly Catholic country, Semana Santa (Holy Week) brings a week of religious ceremonies and special masses commemorating the crucifixion and resurrection of Jesus Christ, with processions of wooden statues through the streets, often accompanied with the music of *chicheros* (brass bands). Leading up to Semana Santa is La Cuaresma (Lent), forty days during which Catholics traditionally abstain from meat. On Fridays during Lent, communities across Nicaragua reenact the Via Crucis, the Fourteen Stations of the Cross, with some devotees dressed as Roman soldiers while others drag heavy wooden crosses as an act of penitence and expression of faith to remember Christ's sufferings.

The annual Via Crucis Acuático features a flotilla of boats decorated with religious statues, flowers, fruits, and fish that marks the stations of the cross by visiting fourteen islands in Las Isletas, near Granada.

The most colorful tradition takes place in the indigenous community of Sutiaba, just outside the city of León, where local families make *alfombras* (literally, carpets), which tell the story of the Passion of Christ in pictures created from layers of colored sawdust.

Other notable celebrations include a pilgrimage of gaily decorated ox-carts that sets out from the town of Nandaime two weeks before Semana Santa and slowly makes its way to San Jorge in Rivas to the Shrine of Nuestro Señor del Rescate de Popoyuapa. Whole families take part in the pilgrimage, often in thanks for prayers answered.

Domingo de Palma (Palm Sunday) marks the official start of Semana Santa, with the faithful carrying palm fronds. In Managua and other cities and towns there is a procession, led by a life-sized statue of Jesus seated upon a donkey, known as the Procesión de la Burrita commemorating the triumphal entry of Jesus into Jerusalem.

Easter Food

All through Lent and Holy Week, Nicaraguans prepare delicious dishes that follow the Catholic traditions of abstaining from meat. *Sopa de queso* is a rich and hearty cheese and maize dough soup topped with crunchy fritters; *arroz con gaspar* is a salted fish and rice dish; and *almibar* is a sweet compote of local fruits cooked in syrup.

On Viernes Santo (Good Friday), some churches hold a Santo Entierro (Holy Burial), in which a casket holding a statue of Jesus is solemnly paraded to the church, with a funeral march played by *chicheros*. This is also a day for reenactments of the Stations of the Cross.

Easter concludes with Domingo de Resurrección (Easter Sunday), a joyous celebration of the resurrection, when statues of Jesus and the Virgin Mary are traditionally brought together.

Not everybody throngs to the nation's churches. Many head to rivers and waterfalls to escape the heat and bathe, and the beaches are packed.

Alegría por la Vida Carnaval (April/May)

Nicaraguans don't have a strong carnival tradition like the one in Brazil, but the Alegría por la Vida (Joy for Life) street party that takes place in the huge plaza in front of the Old Cathedral in Managua probably comes closest. Illuminated by the neon lights of Managua's steel trees, colorful floats led by beauty queens and followed by glitter-covered dancers parade along the main avenue down to the *malecon*, the lakeside promenade, while live music from all over Nicaragua fills the capital from dawn to dusk.

Maypole (May)

The British may have brought the genteel May Day tradition of dancing around a maypole with ribbons to Nicaragua, but in Bluefields they have taken things up a notch. Maypole is a boozy Afro-Caribbean street *fiesta* that lasts a month, with carnival-style parades, battling sound systems, neighborhood block parties into the early hours, and a final blowout in the communities of Old Bank and Punta Fria to the tropical beats of the Tulululu dance.

Baile de Los Chinegros (June 26)

The small town of San Juan de Oriente, one of the Pueblos Blancos near Masaya, is famous for its skilled artisans and burnished ceramics, but it is also home to one of Nicaragua's most unusual folk festivals. Every year, on June 26, the statue of San Juan Bautista (St. John the Baptist), the town's patron saint, is paraded through the streets while young men called Chinegros (because of their blackened faces) brandish bulls' penises made into swords to test their mettle against all comers. An ancient Nicaraguan tradition, which has been linked with pre-Columbian bloodletting rituals, it has strict rules. A man in a horse costume, known as La Yeguita, separates the fighters if the whipping and blows become too intense, and *chicha bruja* (fermented maize hooch) is drunk to deaden the stinging pain of the short bouts. San Juan de Oriente is not the only place that Chinegros fight with bull penis swords, but it is certainly the most famous.

Día de la Revolución (July 19)

Known as Revolution Day, Liberation Day, or Triumph of the Popular Sandinista Revolution, this celebration remembers the day in 1979 that the Sandinista rebels, having taken control of Managua and toppled the Somoza dictatorship, held a triumphant party in the huge square in front of the old cathedral. People come from all over the country to take part in the celebrations in Managua, which feature revolutionary anthems, marching bands, parades, and folk dances.

Crab Soup Festival (August 27-29)

For Nicaragua's Caribbean Corn Islanders the biggest party of the year comes during the Emancipation Day celebrations that mark the moment in 1841 when slavery was finally abolished. On August 27, the locals on Big Corn cook up a rich stew of blue crabs, plantains, and *yuca* (cassava) that is shared out to all present. Festivities include parades, the election of a beauty queen, horse races, live music, and dancing. According to local lore, Queen Victoria abolished slavery in all British territories in the Caribbean in 1838, but it wasn't until August 1841 that Colonel Alexander McDonald, the superintendent of British Honduras, dropped anchor off Long Beach on Big Corn Island to bring the news to the ninety-eight slaves on the island that they were free. Big Corn islanders continue the party on August 29, when a traditional "Crossover" trip to Little Corn Island celebrates the day the slaves there were brought the good news.

Fiestas Patrias (September)

A series of patriotic celebrations marking Central American independence run into each other through September in a swirling sea of blue and white as schoolkids, led by baton-twirling majorettes and marching bands, parade through towns and cities to a cacophony of drums and brass. As part of the celebrations a torch of liberty is ceremonially taken along the Panamerican Highway from Guatemala to Costa Rica, arriving in Nicaragua on September 11 and leaving the country through Costa Rica on September 13. September 14 commemorates the Battle of San Jacinto in 1856, when local fighters delivered the first defeat to William Walker's mercenary army at the San Jacinto hacienda near Tipitapa. The festivities conclude on September 15 with Central American Independence Day, when Costa Rica, El Salvador, Guatemala, Honduras, and Nicaragua all celebrate the day on 1821 when the five nations broke free from Spanish rule.

Columbus is Out, Indigenous Ancestors Are In

Celebrating Columbus Day on October 12, to mark the day in 1492 that Christopher Columbus is said to have arrived in the Americas, is no longer considered politically correct in most countries of Latin America, given the subsequent conquest, killing, forced conversion, and cruel treatment of indigenous Americans by the Spanish conquistadors. This has led some countries to adopt the term "Día de la Raza" (Race Day), with less emphasis on Columbus and a greater focus on events that celebrate the survival of indigenous groups and their culture, history, and traditions. In Nicaragua, the day has been renamed "Día de la Resistencia Indígena," and commemorates Nicaragua's ancient and current indigenous groups with festivities highlighting folk dances, such as El Güegüense, and featuring popular dishes such as *nacatamales* and *indio viejo* (see pages 99 and 100).

Los Agüizotes (Last Friday in October)

All the scary characters of Nicaragua's myths and legends take to the streets of Monimbó in Masaya for the annual procession of Los Agüizotes on the last Friday in October. The name is derived from the Nahuatl words *ahui* (water) and *zotl* (horror). Sometimes called Nicaragua's Halloween, the festival is part of the celebrations in honor of San Jeronimo, Masaya's patron saint. Masked revelers, dressed as horned devils, and local spooks, including La Cegua (the horse-faced woman), El Cadejo (the demon dog), La Llorona (the weeping woman), and the Padre sin Cabeza (the headless priest), hold candles and torches and shuffle through the town to the sound of *chicheros.* The festive spirit continues into the early hours with lashings of *guaro* and Toña beer.

Día de los Fieles Difuntos (Day of the Faithful Departed, November 2)

As in other Catholic countries of the region, Nicaraguans mark the Day of the Dead by remembering the lives of deceased relations. They visit the graves, tidy and clean them, and decorate them with colorful wreaths of fresh flowers. The churches welcome large congregations, and in some cemeteries Catholic priests give a special Mass dedicated to the departed. Some families pay musicians to play at the graveside. Traditional food includes *buñuelos,* fried balls of *yuca* dough mixed with cheese served with honey or syrup, and *sopa borracha* ("drunk soup"), which is actually a sponge cake made with rum.

Garifuna Day (November 19)

The International Garifuna Festival commemorates the arrival of the Afro-Caribbean Garifuna people from St. Vincent to the Central American countries of Guatemala, Belize, Honduras, and Nicaragua in 1797. Week-long celebrations of drumming, dancing, and cultural activities traditionally begin in Bluefields and then move to the small town of Orinoco in Pearl Lagoon, the cultural heart of the Garifuna community in Nicaragua. And there's local firewater, such as the medicinal rum-based brew known as *gifiti.*

In 2001 UNESCO recognized Garifuna dance, language, and music as a Masterpiece of the Oral and Intangible Heritage of Humanity. Closer links and cultural exchanges among the Garifuna communities in Central America have driven a revival of the Garifuna language, punta music, and the *hunguhungu* dance.

Navidad La Gritería, Purisma (December 7 and 8)
La Gritería ("The Yelling") is a loud and joyous festival in honor of the Virgin Mary that takes place on the eve of the Purisima, the Catholic feast that celebrates the Immaculate Conception. In cities and towns all over Nicaragua, people decorate altars outside their houses or on street corners or parks with statues of the Virgin Mary at their center. Festivities often begin at the local church with the pealing of the bells and the first fireworks as the cry goes up: "*Quien causa tanta alegría?*" ("Who causes so much joy?"), and the crowd responds: "*La Concepción de María!*"

This is a full-on fiesta marking the start of the Christmas season, with Christmas food, rum and beer, singing, and lots of fireworks. In the city of León, where the festival originated, the Gritería lasts a week. There is a similar festivity, known as La Gritería de Penitencia, or La Gritería de Chiquita, on the night of August 14 to mark the time that intercessions to the Virgin Mary in 1947, on the eve of the Assumption, miraculously calmed eruptions from the Cerro Negro volcano.

Navidad (Christmas, December 24 and 25)
Christmas is a key event in the Catholic calendar, and the birth of Jesus Christ is celebrated in masses and nativity plays in churches and schools. Masses leading up to December 24 are called *novenas*, and include the singing of *villancicos* (Christmas carols). Everywhere you'll see *pesebres* (nativity scenes), with figures of Joseph and Mary, shepherds, animals, and

the three kings around the manger. These can range from small wooden figures in people's homes to life-size mannequins in public squares. It is traditional in many homes not to put El Niño Jesus (the Baby Jesus) in the manger until Nochebuena (Christmas Eve).

Papa Noel (Father Christmas) is an increasing presence in commercial representations of Christmas, and many Nicaraguan children now write letters to him asking for gifts rather than to El Niño Jesus, as was the custom in the past. Presents are put under the Christmas tree or next to the *pesebre* on Christmas Eve. Most families eat a late dinner, which may include turkey or chicken—but almost always *nacatamales*—and which will be a big sit-down meal with rum and beer. The other major tradition is to go to church for the Misa del Gallo (Midnight Mass), which is always full to bursting in cities and villages alike, with *villancicos* sung to the accompaniment of fireworks set off in the streets.

Día de Navidad (Christmas Day) is a time to open presents, visit family, and enjoy another big meal.

SUPERSTITIONS AND BELIEFS
Given the continuation of indigenous beliefs from pre-Columbian and existing indigenous groups, the legacy of Spanish culture from the days of the conquest, and the influence of Catholicism, Nicaragua has a rich blend of superstitions and myths that we can cover only briefly here. A fear of black cats, and the idea that the number thirteen is unlucky—especially a thirteenth day of the month falling on a *Viernes* (Friday) or sometimes *Martes* (Tuesday) —are widespread superstitions brought from Europe.

The indigenous *cosmovision* (world view) centered on the idea that all things are interlinked is continued today mostly among the Miskito, Sumo, and Rama, although ancient beliefs relating to the arrival of the rains and the best time to harvest persist among country-dwellers.

The most persistent superstitions relate to folk tales of spooky characters such as La Cegua, a woman with the face of a horse who comes out at night to prey on men who are far from home, perhaps drinking or being unfaithful, and La Carreta Nagua, a ghostly carriage drawn by skeleton horses and driven by the Grim Reaper, which is thought to herald a death.

TRADITIONAL PRODUCTS AND CRAFTS

Nicaragua is famous for the exceptional quality of its mountain-grown coffee, award-winning cigars, and super-smooth Flor de Caña rum, which has been produced in Chichigalpa by the Pellas family for more than a hundred years. Handicrafts include carved wooden ornaments, ceramics, masks, basketry, and

cotton goods, produced by artisans in much the same way as they have been made for centuries. The country's main crafts market is the Mercado Viejo (Old Market) in Masaya, and from here it is possible to visit the family-run workshops of the artisans in the surrounding Pueblos Blancos.

The attractive burnished pottery with geometrical and animal designs produced in San Juan de Oriente —one of the Pueblos Blancos— continues a local tradition that stretches back before the arrival of the Spanish. Many of the potters have adapted age-old designs to cater to modern tastes, and produce a wide range of colorful pieces, including wind chimes, flower pots, and decorative plates. Famous craftsmen, such as Gregorio Bracamonte and the UNESCO-heralded maestro Helio Gutierrez, take inspiration from their pre-Columbian past and produce beautifully detailed replicas of Mayan- and Aztec-influenced archaeological pieces.

Nicaragua is also famed for its hand-woven hammocks, made from cotton colored with natural dyes and with trademark fringes. You can find good-quality hammocks in Granada at a social project aimed at giving employment opportunities for deaf youngsters. The NGO founded by Tio Antonio, a Spaniard from Valencia called Antonio Prieto Buñuel, also runs Café de las Sonrisas, the first sign-language coffee shop in the Americas staffed entirely by deaf servers and chefs.

The utopian artists' colony set up in the Solentiname Islands in the 1960s by the revolutionary poet and priest Ernesto Cardenal gave birth to a primitivist art movement, which has brought international acclaim. The naive style of Solentiname art was strongly influenced by the Managua-based painter Róger Pérez de la Rocha, and features Eden-like depictions of dense rainforests teeming with bird and animal life indigenous to the islands.

chapter four

MAKING FRIENDS

Latin Americans of all countries are generally portrayed in the media as smiling, salsa-dancing, and sociable. Nicaraguans do share the warm and friendly characteristics of their tropical cousins in Central and South America, but, especially in the case of those living in the rural areas of the northern hills, can be more reserved on first meeting foreigners who don't speak Spanish. Break the ice, however, and they are some of the friendliest people you'll ever meet.

HOSPITALITY
The Nicaraguans are used to helping each other out when times get tough, and many friendships are forged

from solidarity and mutual aid. Generous hospitality is a trait that characterizes people from all parts of the country, despite the economic constraints they face.

It can be a humbling experience to visit a poor rural home and be offered a meal and a bed for the night by people who clearly have very little and are asking for nothing in return, but it would be considered rude to refuse. Think how you can best repay your hosts, but don't embarrass them by offering cash. Providing something for their children's education would be appreciated, or you could take them out for a meal.

FRIENDSHIP

Travelers and volunteers find it easy to strike up friendships with the people they meet. Nicaraguans love to hang out and share a good-natured laugh and a joke, although deeper friendships, as anywhere in the world, take longer to form.

Most Nicaraguans have a social circle that centers principally on the family and then extends to neighbors, school friends, and coworkers. Friends may be invited home for a special event such as a birthday party, christening, or wedding, but generally friends meet up away from the house. Foreigners working in Nicaragua can expect to be invited by Nicaraguan coworkers to join them for an after-work drink or a meal out, which is a good first step toward making friends. If you turn the offer down you might be thought standoffish.

An invitation home to meet the family is a significant compliment. Make sure to take a gift—perhaps something from your country, or some beer or rum, if you know your hosts drink. Whatever the social setting, bear in mind that all attempts you make to speak Spanish, try new food, join in the dancing, and have fun will be greatly appreciated. Failure to join in will see you labeled *aguado* (watery), *banano* (banana), or an *aguafiestas* (killjoy, or party pooper).

When In Nicaragua, Do As the Locals Do

The Nicaraguans are friendly and sociable, but they are also very respectful of visitors to their country. If you don't speak to them, or give only monosyllabic answers to their questions, or stick like glue to your fellow traveling companions, they will assume you aren't interested in making friends. To break the ice you'll need to be proactive, make eye contact, smile, and use the Spanish words you know.

Just as they do themselves, make a point of saying *Buenos días* (Good day), *Buenas tardes* (Good afternoon), or *Buenas noches* (Good evening) when you walk into a room or meet people in the street. Get used to saying *Hola!* (Hi!) to everybody. Introduce yourself with a simple phrase like *Mi nombre es …* (my name is …), ask people for their names *Y tu?* (And you?), and remember them for next time. As your confidence improves, throw in some Nica-speak to show your appreciation—words like *tuani* or *diacachimba*, which both mean cool, or great. For more on Nica-speak, or *Nicañol*, see pages 154 and 156.

CONVERSATION STARTERS AND STOPPERS

The Nicaraguans live most of their lives on the street, and are highly sociable. When it gets too hot they relax in front of the house in rocking chairs, shooting the breeze with their neighbors, or sit in the local plaza with friends. They like to socialize in groups and keep conversations light, focusing on things they have in common. In such a group, you can expect questions about your family, your favorite music, food, and beer. You will also be asked what you think about Nicaragua.

Considering how proud people are of their country, and how hard they have fought in the past to battle tyrants and tempests, and especially given the difficult history Nicaragua has had with the USA, launching into a critique of the country will not be well received. While locals might gripe about the traffic in Managua, local politics, or the problems of finding work, they won't appreciate a foreign visitor doing the same. It's a question of respect.

THE DATING GAME

Buscando amor (looking for love) is hard enough at home, without all the cultural nuances involved of being in a new country with a different culture and a different language. In Nicaragua, girls start having families young, people live at home until they get married, and in general the dating game is still quite traditional and macho. Just as in dancing a cumbia, when it comes to love men are expected to lead. The positive side of this old-school approach is manifested in the general courtesies and gallantry shown to women. A man is expected to open doors for a woman, pay for everything on a night out, and make sure she is delivered safely to her door. A woman can expect to receive flowery declarations and effusive compliments (*piropos*). A less positive aspect is the possessiveness and jealousies that sometimes ensue.

In big towns and cities younger Nicaraguans are increasingly looking for love via their smartphones, on apps like Tinder. Dating Web sites can also be a useful way to line up dates, but steer clear of the ones that specifically want to match local women with foreign men, as they tend to be less about romance and more about business.

The best way to *ligar* (hook up) in Nicaragua is probably to follow the same advice for finding friends:

go out and meet people. Nicaraguans are happy to play matchmaker, and if you build up a group of local friends—especially at a language school, volunteering project, or workplace—they will soon start introducing you to possible soul mates. Nicaraguans like going out in groups, which takes the pressure out of that first date, and if you don't find romance at least you've expanded your social circle.

THE LANGUAGE BARRIER

If you are visiting the Corn Islands or Bluefields the local Creole sounds very similar to the lilting English you will find throughout the Caribbean. For the rest of Nicaragua, however, the more Spanish you can speak, the greater chance you will have of striking up conversations, joining in the fun, and making friends. A phrase book or translation App is not much use in a noisy bar, and resorting to miming what you want is a fun way to get involved but can get tiring. Whatever your level of Spanish, Nicaraguans will use all the English they have to make things easier, and still include you in social events, but it's harder to click with people when you don't even have the basics.

One way to ease your way into Nicaraguan society and culture is to take Spanish classes—a great way to practice and pick up local vocabulary, which will boost your confidence. There are some good Spanish schools, and prices are very low compared to studying in Spain and other Latin American countries.

Classes also provide a place to make friends with fellow learners, your teacher, and, in a home-stay, your host family, who will be able to put you on a fast track to the best places to eat and the hottest hangouts in town. Try to arrive armed with all the Spanish you can muster, and note down popular Nicaraguan words and phrases that will help you fit in. (See Chapter 9.)

"Dale Pues, Chele!"

Starting from childhood and on through school, Nicaraguans love to give each other nicknames. So just as a kid called William in the US or the UK might end up as Billy, Bill, or Will, in Nicaragua the names Francisco, Jesus, and Eduardo are shortened to Pancho, Chucho, and Lalo respectively, Enrique becomes Quique, and Concepción becomes Conchita.

Nicknames tend to start in the family home and can stick with a person for life. Many poke fun at the person, often picking up on an aspect of their physical appearance, which depending on the delivery can be offensive in an argument or endearing among friends. In Granada, the most famous stallholders selling the city's signature dish *vigorón* are known by their nicknames (see page 60). Obviously you have big feet if you are called "Pata de Nacatamal," referring to the large local corn dish wrapped in a banana leaf.

Foreigners are not exempt from this national love of nicknames. While it's unusual to hear the word *gringo* to refer to English-speaking or European foreigners, you will hear the word *chele* (masculine) or *chela* (feminine) everywhere you go, often in the diminutive form of *chelito/chelita*, to make it sound sweeter. The word is an anagram of *leche* (milk), and is used to refer to anybody—foreign or Nicaraguan—who is blond or light-skinned. A popular logo you'll see all over Nicaragua on T-shirts is *Dale pues, chele!* (Go for it, White Boy!).

NICA TIME OR *HORA BRITÁNICO?*

One of the first adjustments you'll need to make on arrival in Nicaragua is to the local sense of time, or punctuality, which locals refer to as "Nica time," and which can add anything from half an hour or an hour to an arranged meeting time. This fluid interpretation of time can be frustrating to newcomers, but you'll soon understand why timekeeping is less rigid when you've experienced the energy-sapping heat of midday, been stuck in gridlocked Managua traffic for an hour, or been confined to your hotel by a sudden tropical downpour.

Nica time also includes the social obligation to stop and chat with family and friends on the street, and is wrapped up with the general philosophy of enjoying the moment and adapting to situations as they occur, rather than being obsessed with getting somewhere on the dot. In fact, arriving at social engagements like a Swiss clock will not win you any friends. Turn up at somebody's door at the appointed time, and you are likely to find your hosts are still getting ready. Even at weddings, christenings, and funerals, people tend to turn up at least half an hour late.

Rather than fussing and fighting over Nica time, it's better to relax and embrace it from day one. If you want to meet somebody at 8:00 p.m., arrange the date for

7:30, and don't be upset if they turn up at 9:00. When somebody tells you the time of a meeting, ask "Is that Nica time or *Hora Britanico* (British time)?" At least you'll get a smile.

WHAT TO WEAR

Nicaragua is hot—very hot in some places—so light, informal dress is the order of the day. For men, even for business meetings, a light linen long-sleeved *guayabera* shirt worn with smart pants is acceptable, and is a good way to beat the heat. Women can wear skirts or pants to work. Nicaraguans take great pride in their appearance.

In beach towns, cover up with a T-shirt and long shorts or pants before entering a local church, bank, office, or market. It is considered disrespectful to step into a place of worship in a bikini or super-short shorts, and you should remove your hat when entering a church.

Topless bathing is not considered acceptable on public beaches. Most Nicaraguans have a conservative attitude when it comes to how much flesh they flash. Their Catholic roots run deep, and going topless on a beach that attracts families with children could cause offense. If you do see a woman topless, she is more likely to be a foreign tourist than a local.

THE EXPAT LIFE

Nicaragua's reputation as the safest country in the region, combined with cheaper living costs and improved infrastructure and amenities, means that increasing numbers of North Americans and Europeans are choosing to relocate here instead, either permanently or just when the weather turns cold at home. The main expat areas are the colonial cities of Granada and León, the Pacific beach town of San Juan del Sur, the tobacco city of Estelí, the coffee towns of Matagalpa and Jinotepe, and the Corn Islands. Managua also has a sizeable foreign community of diplomatic staff, executives working for multinationals, and representatives of NGOs and volunteer groups. In 2017 International Living ranked Nicaragua eighth in its list of top ten countries to retire to, scoring it highly for buying and renting, cost of living, and healthy lifestyle.

Not surprisingly, there are a number of social groups set up by foreign nationals that you can join to widen your social circle, find work, or pick up tips on running a business. The international social networking group InterNations has a chapter in Managua, and offers young and not so young expats the opportunity to meet old hands and locals at various events. There are also Facebook groups for expats that run get-togethers, pub quizzes, language exchanges, and Latin dance nights for the English-speaking community.

VOLUNTEERING

One of the best ways to break out of the tourist bubble, meet Nicaraguans, and make new friends is to get involved in educational or social projects as a volunteer. Things may be improving in Nicaragua, but it's still the second-poorest country in the Western Hemisphere, and positive contributions by foreign visitors can have a great impact on small communities. Spending time with a local community digging a well to bring fresh water to a village, lending a hand in painting a rural school, and helping out with English lessons are rewarding ways to get close to the people. For those wanting to get involved in longer projects there are rural home-stays that offer the opportunity to get under the skin of a Nicaraguan community, learn about the life, improve your Spanish, give something back, and make lifelong friends.

The good thing about volunteering in Nicaragua is that it's easy to organize. Support for social programs is a facet of Nicaraguan life that is linked to Sandinista ideology and the Liberation Theology ideas of the Catholic priests who went to help remote communities in the 1960s. In the 1980s, when the Contra War was at its height, thousands of foreigners came to Nicaragua to help harvest coffee, rebuild schools, plant trees, offer medical assistance in rural towns, and assist the literacy campaign launched by the Sandinista government. Some of these groups were politically inspired, like the Brigadistas from the US, UK, and Europe, who wanted to show their solidarity with the Sandinista Revolution. Other groups were religious in nature, and came as church groups or missionaries to alleviate poverty and help the sick. When Hurricane Mitch devastated the country in 1998, more volunteers came to help out along with international NGOs, who set up permanent programs.

Most tour operators, hotels, hostels, coffee farms, and surf camps catering to foreign tourists can arrange for you to spend a day or a week helping out at a local school or environmental project as part of your trip.

The Nicaragua Solidarity Campaign in London works with thirteen twin-town groups, schools, and social organizations in the UK that support a wide variety of cultural, educational, and environmental projects, and hundreds of US church groups are involved in volunteering projects.

chapter five

THE NICARAGUANS AT HOME

After three difficult decades in the 1970s, '80s, and '90s, Nicaraguans are finally starting to see material improvements in their daily lives as the economy grows and health, education, and transport services improve.

One of the delights of Nicaragua is that the process of modernization has not occurred at the expense of timeless traditions that are so central to Nicaraguan culture. When it comes to food, for example, the morning routine of making *tortillas* by hand has changed little for centuries. Iconic Nicaraguan dishes like *gallo pinto*, *quesillos*, *nacatamales*, and *güirilas* are as popular today as they always have been. You can find US fast food stores in many cities and towns, but these generally cater to the middle class. For ordinary Nicaraguans a fast-food treat consists of an occasional meal of grilled chicken or pork from a local *fritanga*, a street-side barbecue. It's a cheap way of feeding the family, and gives mothers and grandmothers a break from the kitchen.

With the entry into the country of the US retail giant Walmart, more people shop at supermarkets, but most Nicaraguans buy their essentials at local, family-run stores, and will devotedly visit their local fruit and vegetable market to find what's fresh that day.

Things are gradually changing, of course. These days, a ride in an elegant carriage pulled by a horse decked out in ribbons may be aimed mainly at tourists in the colonial city of Granada, but in market towns like Masaya you will still see ordinary housewives taking their shopping home in a horse and buggy or in a *caponera* (tricycle taxi with a roof).

The survival of so many quaint and colorful traditions is partly due to Nicaragua's long years of isolation and economic stagnation. The Somoza family dictatorship, the US-backed Contra War that followed the Sandinista Revolution, and natural disasters all led to Nicaragua becoming the second-poorest country in the Western Hemisphere, after Haiti. On the positive side, Nicaraguans have steadfastly clung on to the cultural quirks that make them unique, and local dishes, folk music, artistic traditions, and ancient festivals continue to be an integral part of daily life.

Nicaraguans are feeling happier about their lives, according to the World Happiness Report published by the United Nations in 2017. Despite its poverty, it posted the greatest gains in perceived happiness since the UN's last happiness survey, coming in at number 43 out of 155 countries. It scored highly on the social support networks provided by family, neighbors, and friends, and life expectancy rose from 74 years to 75.8 years between 2010 and 2015.

HOUSING

Managua is home to more than a million people, but apart from a few modern malls, large parks, and sparkling new stadiums it can feel more like a provincial town as you drive through neighborhood after neighborhood of single-story houses. Managua was a latecomer as a capital, so lacks the colonial grandeur of Granada and León. There has been no real center to the city since the 1972 earthquake ripped out the heart of the downtown area, toppling nearly all of the tall buildings, although a grand regeneration plan is now transforming the lakeshore area into a major attraction.

The grand families of Managua live in elegant villas known as *quintas,* with manicured lawns, landscaped gardens, and swimming pools, or the kind of ultra-modern condos you might find in Miami. Along the road to Masaya and next to the shiny new malls that are restoring the capital's luster, new residential areas are a reflection of the country's growing middle class.

In historic Granada, one of the oldest cities in the Americas, the rich once lived in large, two-story, neo-colonial mansions brightly painted in pastel shades with rooms set around a central courtyard and separate quarters for servants. Some of these old mansions in the streets around the canary-yellow

cathedral have been converted into elegant boutique hotels, giving tourists the opportunity to experience the grand life of the nineteenth-century traders who once lived there. Granada, like the beach town of San Juan del Sur, is also home to a large expat community, and the influx of foreigners looking for retirement properties has seen a corresponding boom in real estate prices.

In León, a former capital, the city center is also dominated by colonial buildings, many of them converted into apartments. A visit to El Convento, a former convent that now operates as a luxury hotel, gives a glimpse into the way wealthy Nicaraguans decorate their colonial homes, with antique icons and contemporary art. It also has a plunge pool for escaping the city heat.

Outside the cities, where the majority of Nicaraguans live, humble houses made of adobe or breeze blocks with ceramic tile or corrugated zinc roofs are the norm. Homes in remote areas still lack electricity and have latrines rather than plumbed-in bathroom facilities. Many families still have to pump water from deep wells, adding an extra chore to their daily existence.

To supplement their diet, Nicaraguans plant fruit trees around the house, cultivate food plants like squashes and herbs, and keep chickens and pigs. Cooking, even in towns, is still done on a *fogón,* an open fire or wood-burning stove, often located to one side of the house. In rural areas you might see a whole family helping to carry firewood home, or horses or oxen pulling carts piled high with wood to sell.

On the Atlantic coast, in Miskito and Garifuna communities, and along the Pacific coast, are wooden houses on stilts known as *tambos.* Raising the house

gives protection from rainy-season floods and provides shelter for livestock. Picturesque thatched roofs can still be found on coastal and rural houses, but are gradually being replaced by zinc.

Wherever Nicaraguans live, on a cobblestone street in colonial Granada, or in a tiny rural village of a few houses, when dusk starts to fall you will generally find people sitting outside their houses, catching up on gossip with friends and neighbors and taking advantage of the evening breeze.

DAILY LIFE

For most Nicaraguans the day starts early—sometimes very early. Market traders bring in their wares at the crack of dawn to set up before the first customers arrive, and fishermen arrive with their first catch of the day just as dawn breaks.

Many Nicaraguan mothers are up before the roosters crow to prepare fresh tortillas for the family breakfast. A light *desayuno* (breakfast) might be a tortilla with *cuajada* (cheese curd) and a sweet black coffee. A full Nica breakfast almost always includes *gallo pinto* (rice and beans), usually with *huevos* (eggs), *crema* (cream), *queso frito* (fried cheese), and *platanos fritos* (fried plantains). Those in a hurry will pick up a street snack on the way to work.

HOME HELP

Rich families in Nicaragua may rely on the services of a mini-army of uniformed maids, cooks, nannies, chauffeurs, and gardeners to keep their pampered lives running smoothly, but most middle-class Nicaraguans will also have somebody who comes in to help with cleaning, cooking, shopping, or child care. Even in less affluent communities, neighbors may take in washing or mending to supplement their income, and in rural areas it is not uncommon for cooperatives run by women to share childcare duties to free up other members for work.

For expats unused to the Latin American world of live-in maids, hiring someone to help you at home can be a challenge. While treating your domestic workers with respect, it is essential to be quite clear about what you require. Follow Nicaraguan labor laws on minimum wage and social security payments, whether your helpers live with the family or come in to work on certain days. Agencies that specialize in finding domestic workers can provide references from past employers and give advice, but it's a good idea to seek recommendations from other foreigners also. Dedicated pages set up for expats on Facebook are a good place to get tips.

Children have to be at school by 7:00 a.m., and a typical sight in towns and villages is a parent on a bike with a uniformed child sitting across the crossbar as they are taken to school or brought home at lunchtime. Crowded buses take workers from the satellite towns around the cities to their jobs. Offices start work by 8:00 a.m., the time when most shops start to open.

When it comes to *almuerzo* (lunch), many people eat out. The food courts in Managua's malls are full at lunchtime, and workers often head to a *comedor* (a hole-in-the-wall eatery) in the local market that serves an inexpensive set menu. Individual workers might take in sandwiches or order a simple hot meal to be delivered to their factory or office from a local food stall. *Gallo pinto* is as popular for lunch as it is for breakfast.

The working day for most people is over by 5:00 or 6:00 p.m. Mothers and grandmothers, who do most of the cooking, will pick up a few things on the way home for the *cena* (evening meal), which is generally quite light. Bringing friends back to eat with the family is not very common, so if you do get an invitation to dinner this is a privilege.

Nicaraguans do a fair amount of socializing when the sun goes down, even if it's just a visit to a local church, a promenade around town, or a trip to the park to check their Facebook page using the free Wi-Fi. On weekends, after a few drinks at a bar or *discoteca*, the late-night action usually comes to an end at a street-side *fritanga* serving barbecued meats and savory snacks drizzled with chili sauce.

A MOTHER'S LOVE

With the men often gone all day, or working far from home, it's the women who hold households together in Nicaragua. Mothers, grandmothers, aunts, godmothers, and sisters are typically the ones who manage household finances, cook and clean, look after the babies, help with school projects, and take on second jobs to bring in extra cash. When mothers have to work, grandmothers or daughters take their place in front of the family stove. A typical early-morning sound in Nicaragua is "hand-clapping," as balls of maize dough are formed into tortillas, sometimes by three generations of women together. Large families can function only when everybody pulls together, and it's the women who organize big family get-togethers, often roping in neighbors to help.

Given the central role of women in Nicaraguan culture, it is no surprise that the Virgin Mary, the very epitome of motherly sacrifice for Catholics, is the focus of such fervent devotion, especially during La Gritería and the Purisima, the December festivals in her honor.

Nicaraguan women are strong, forged by the country's difficult past, and determined to provide a better future for their children.

DAILY SHOPPING

Most people in Nicaragua continue to do their food
shopping locally. Known simply as *una venta,* the
simplest form of store is just a house where a family
makes a few things to sell from the window. Typical
products are *posicles* (popsicles), *queque* (cake), and
cuajada (cheese curd). *Nacatamales* are traditionally
eaten on Sunday mornings, along with a black coffee
to aid digestion. The families who make them produce
a hundred at a time, putting up a sign on a Thursday
and selling out by Friday.

The next step up from a *venta* is a *pulpería*—a
general store piled high with everything from candies
and canned sardines to soda pop, soap powder, shoes,
and shampoo. In some you can get a cold beer and a
fresh local cigar, and in others you can have your pick
of buckets and baskets. No two *pulperías* seem to stock
the same things, making them endlessly fascinating
to browse around. Often, a *pulpería* is just the front
of a house that has been converted into a store, but
some are like modern mini-supermarkets. Larger

convenience stores with a greater range of products on sale are more likely to be called *misceláneas,* but the terms are virtually synonymous in most cases, and *pulperías* and *misceláneas* are very much at the heart of the communities they serve. Open and covered markets also play an important part in daily life, providing fruit, vegetables, and consumer goods at cheaper prices, and as a generator of income for the stallholders.

At the other end of the scale, large shopping malls, like the super-swish Galerías Santo Domingo in Managua, offer the middle classes high-end stores, in-mall supermarkets, pharmacies, large food courts, cinemas, restaurants, and bars, all under one roof.

MARVELOUS MARKETS

Managua has two vast markets. Fruit and vegetables, fish and meat, dried grains and chilies, clothes and shoes, toys and TVs—it might be easier to list the things you can't buy in these sprawling labyrinths. For a flavor of the largest market in the Americas, tuck away your valuables and head to Managua's mammoth Mercado Oriental. Steel yourself for a complete sensory overload as you delve into this city within a city, a great maze of covered passages filled to the bursting point with every imaginable type of merchandise and an army of insistent vendors.

If you're looking for an authentic taste of Nicaragua and a bit of culture without the crush, the Mercado Roberto Huembes, next to Managua's main bus station, has an extensive selection of arts and crafts from all over the country, and sit-down food stalls serving a selection of Nicaragua's tastiest traditional treats.

In Masaya, the cultural heart of Nicaragua, tourists are usually taken to the *Mercado Viejo* (Old Market), also known as the Mercado de Artesanías (Craft Market). It's an attractive space where folk music and occasional dance displays add to the ambience as you browse through the psychedelically colored primitivist paintings, balsa-wood birds, and *diacachimba!* (cool!) T-shirts. For the same selection of handicrafts, with the bonus of visiting a bustling local market, head up Calle Mercado to the Mercado Municipal and try the nationally famous food stalls.

If you want to see how the locals live in Granada, a visit to the market is a must. Iconic dishes such as *vigorón* are served on a banana leaf and accompanied with a bright-purple pithaya, or pitahaya (dragon fruit) juice that comes in a plastic bag with a straw. Stalls selling chili sauce from vast tubs, or piled high with fresh fish from Cocibolca (Lake Nicaragua), are perfect for an Instagram shot—but ask before snapping away.

Nicaraguans haggle when shopping in markets, but foreigners should keep in mind that vendors don't make vast fortunes from their stalls—most earn just enough to feed their families. A dogged insistence on saving every possible córdoba when making a purchase can come across as rude. A cheeky smile may get you a better discount.

EDUCATION

There's a real passion for education in Nicaragua. Step out on to the streets of any town or village, and you'll see children in crisply pressed white shirts hurrying to school. Free education and assistance with school materials, offered by the state, from preschool to high school, have helped the country to improve literacy and encouraged more students to continue their education to technical college or university.

Some schools do two shifts, but most students are out of school by lunchtime—which is another reason for grandparents and extended family to pitch in to share cooking and child care duties. The school year runs from February to November.

The School System

Compulsory free education in the public school system currently starts in *primaria* (primary school) for children from five to twelve, although in many areas it is available to three- and four-year-olds at *pre-escolar* (preschool). *Secundaria* (secondary school, or junior high) is from thirteen to fifteen, and is also obligatory. *Prepa* (*preparatoria*) is the equivalent of high school, and prepares students for entry into a technical college or university. This level is not compulsory, and the reality is that most young people leave at the end of secondary school, and some before that. Both public and private schools have to follow the curriculum laid down by MINED (Ministerio de Educación, Education Ministry), but private schools can offer extra subjects and often have after-school classes or sports that extend the school day. For middle- and upper-class Nicaraguans, attending a good school, getting a place at a good university, and doing a Masters or MBA abroad are seen as the keys to a good career.

In 2018, primary schools across the country started teaching English for the first time, in response to a government initiative to equip students with a foreign language that would be useful for business and tourism.

MILITARY SERVICE

In 1983, during the Contra War, when the country was under attack by US-backed right-wing paramilitary forces based in Honduras, the Sandinista government brought in conscription for all men aged between eighteen and forty. Compulsory military service ended with the signing of the peace accords in 1990. Military service is now voluntary and open to all Nicaraguan men and women aged between eighteen and thirty who have passed Sixth Grade and want to serve in the country's army, air force, or navy.

THE CYCLE OF FAMILY LIFE

For rich and poor alike there is a cycle of family life—a celebration of national and religious holidays, births, baptisms, weddings, birthdays, and *quinceañera* parties (see below)—that brings family and friends together. If you spend any time traveling in Nicaragua, or get a job working alongside Nicaraguans, you might be lucky enough to get an invitation to one of these events. It's certainly worth attending if you want a real insight into Nicaragua and Nicaraguan life.

Milestones Marked by the Catholic Church

El bautizo (baptism), when a child receives Christian names, usually takes place shortly after birth at a Church service attended by family and close friends. This a joyous occasion, with gifts, and, typically, a post-baptism party with food, drink, and music.

Primera Comunión (First Communion) is when young Catholics aged seven to twelve first take the consecrated wafer and wine that symbolize the body and blood of Christ, during Mass. Typically gathered in a group for the celebration, boys and girls dress in white, with white gloves and white candles symbolizing purity. Boys often wear long-sleeved *guayabera* shirts, and girls wear veils or floral headbands.

Confirmación (Confirmation) takes place at around fifteen or sixteen years of age, when young adults confirm their faith at a special Mass.

Sweet Fifteen

A major event for young Nicaraguan girls is the *fiesta de quince años* (fifteenth-birthday party), which is seen as a rite of passage into womanhood. The elaborate celebrations are more like a wedding than a Sweet Sixteen party in the US. Depending on the budget, the *quinceañera* (literally, the fifteen-year-old girl) dresses up in a ballgown with a crown or tiara, attended by her closest friends in formal suits and dresses. Traditionally, a *quince* starts with a Mass in church; photographs are taken on the church steps; and then there is the party. The *quinceañera* dances a waltz with her father; then there is a toast, perhaps a serenade by a *mariachi* band, and then a live band or DJ plays on into the night. *Quinceañera* presents can be as extravagant as the party. At one time a trip to the US was all the rage for the daughters of the rich; nowadays presents can be a tour around Europe, or a car.

For poorer families the party will be at home. The dress might be homemade, but everybody tries to make the day special for the *quinceañera*.

Weddings

There are few festive occasions in Nicaragua as joyous, colorful, or costly as a wedding. A church wedding can be an extravagant affair for those who can afford it, with a ceremony in a historic colonial church, a myriad maids of honor, and a fairytale horse and carriage for the couple. For the majority of Nicaraguans, the big day may be less lavish, but people still pull out all the

stops to make it a special occasion, dress up in their Sunday best, and host a party with festive food and drink for guests.

Before a church wedding the couple must have their details notarized at a *registro civil* (register office), but it is more common to be married at home in the presence of a justice of the peace. Before the 2015 Family Code came into force, girls as young as fourteen could marry with their parents' consent, but nowadays they must be sixteen. Without parental consent, the couple must be over eighteen.

The process for foreigners marrying Nicaraguans is quite straightforward, and destination weddings at beautiful beaches along the Pacific coast are now becoming popular as the country opens up to tourism.

Funerals

Just as most important events in the cycle of life are celebrated in common with family and friends in Nicaragua, funerals are no exception. When somebody dies in Nicaragua the family will hold a *vela* (wake) at the family home or in a funeral parlor. Food and hot drinks are provided for the mourners, who are encouraged to accompany the dead person on their last night before burial or cremation. Alcoholic drinks are also served, and the house is opened up to all who want to pay their last respects. In Granada, a typical local sight is the parade of grand funeral carriages passing through the streets on the day of a funeral, sometimes accompanied by hundreds of mourners. Nicaraguans continue to keep the memories alive of those who have passed on, and every year, on November 2, families congregate at the graves of their loved ones on the Día de los Fieles Difuntos (Day of the Faithful Departed; see page 64).

chapter six

TIME OUT

Nicaraguans like to take their leisure time at a leisurely pace. The enjoyment of local dishes and eating out at street stalls and markets is something all can afford, and there are fierce debates over which town—or even which family—produces the best *güirilas* (sweet corn pancakes), *quesillos* (soft-cheese tortilla wraps), or *nacatamales* (see page 99).

There may be only a handful of art galleries in the country, but art is everywhere, from the tropical colors of the folk art sold at markets and hung up at home to the murals that brighten the walls of towns and cities. Back in the 1980s Nicaragua was famed for the murals dedicated to Sandinista heroes and historic events, but nowadays you are more likely to find the surreal

or playful expressions of younger artists influenced by modern graffiti and tagging trends.

While only the larger towns and cities boast movie theaters, Nicaraguans have good access to cable TV and satellite services, and will gather together to watch a new film or set up a screen in the town square to watch the boxing when a local champion is fighting.

Baseball and football are played throughout the country, and surfing is popular on the perfect waves of the Pacific coast. International boxing victories are a source of national pride, and local rivalries dominate the baseball diamonds of every town and village.

Temperatures can soar in the dry months, and people like to spend their free time in the open air, sitting with family and friends outside their houses, where they can beat the heat and shoot the breeze. The roll-out of free Wi-Fi at parks and plazas across the country has also served to perpetuate the timeless tradition of hanging out in the town square.

The annual round of local events features countless *fiestas*, in which masked dances hark back to ancient customs, and the marimba, maracas, and guitar provide the melodies to old folk songs that evoke the beauty of the countryside and the proud resilience of the people.

FOOD

Nicaragua ticks all the boxes for culinary travelers and foodies seeking gastronomic adventures. The food is hearty and filling, and there's a variety of exotic fruits and fruit juices to try—like the dramatically purple pitaya, or dragon fruit, and the little yellow, slightly sharp-tasting *nancites*, or nance fruit. Those looking to eat like a local will find traditional Nicaraguan dishes at high-end hotels, restaurants, hole-in-the-wall eateries, bustling local markets, busy street-corner grills, and humble home-stays. Made from local ingredients and the kind of passion you only get in places where people love to cook and eat, Nicaraguan food is as much an expression of Nica pride as the blue and white stripes of the national flag.

With the growth of tourism, the arrival of expats, and the inexorable spread of US fast-food chains, the culinary choices for those craving Italian-style pizza, Asian-fusion, or plain old burgers and fries are now much greater than they were twenty years ago, especially in larger cities and towns. In popular travel spots such as Granada, León, Estelí, and San Juan del Sur vegetarians can find specialist restaurants and menus offering more than just meals without the meat. This gastronomic globalization cuts both ways: one of the busiest restaurants in Granada is O'Shea's Irish Bar, where locals come to try the cottage pie.

Comida Típica—Traditional Food
Gallo pinto: Much more than rice and beans, *gallo pinto* (speckled rooster) is a national dish that Nicaraguans

happily eat for breakfast, lunch, and dinner. It's made of red beans, white rice, and diced onions, fried together in a large skillet. On the Atlantic coast

and islands the beans, rice, and onions get a Caribbean twist and are fried in coconut oil to make them extra creamy. The local joke is that Nicaragua runs on *gallo-pinto* power.

The full Nica: The *desayuno típico* (traditional breakfast) comes with a generous portion of *gallo pinto* accompanied with *huevos revueltos* (scrambled eggs), *maduros* (fried plantains), *queso frito* (fried cheese), and a fresh maize tortilla. In some places you get *cuajada* (curd cheese), *crema* (sour cream), *pico de gallo*, a vinegary salsa of finely chopped tomatoes and onions, or *moronga* (blood sausage). With a fruit juice such as *sandía* (watermelon) or *calala* (passionfruit) and a strong local coffee, the *desayuno típico* is designed to set you up for a long day.

Nacatamales: This ancient indigenous dish derives its name from *nacatl* (meat) and *tamalli* (something wrapped) from Nahuatl, the language of the ancient Aztecs. Made from maize dough mixed with lard and colored with reddish *achiote* (annatto), they are stuffed with pork, rice, potato, a slice of tomato, and a minty herb called *yerba buena*. The final flourish is to wrap the dough parcels in a plantain leaf and boil them. Take off the plantain leaf before tucking in!

Baho: Beef, *yuca* (cassava), plantains, onions, and peppers are steamed together in a huge cooking pot sealed with layers of banana leaves. Eaten from a banana leaf with a vinegary cabbage slaw, *baho* is a popular weekend indulgence and is said to cure hangovers.

Quesillos: These cheesy treats, sold from street carts, are thick tortillas wrapped around a circle of soft white cheese smothered with *curtido* (finely chopped pickled onion) and a generous dollop of *crema* (sour cream). The towns of La Paz Centro and Nagarote, on the road between León and Managua, both insist that they produce the best *quesillos* in Nicaragua. Add a hearty dash of homemade chili sauce, and accompany your *quesillo* with *tiste*, a drink made of ground cocoa and toasted maize served in a gourd cup.

Vigorón: there's only one place to eat *vigorón*, and that's in Granada, where it was created in 1914. A mini-

mountain of boiled *yuca* and *chicharrones* (pork rinds) topped with a cabbage salad containing slices of *mimbro*, a sharp-tasting fruit from the cucumber tree, it's sold in Granada by street vendors with nicknames like "El Gordito" (the Fat Man), "La Pelona" (the Hairy Woman), and "La Perla" (the Pearl), who all have steadfast fans.

Indio viejo: A stew of shredded beef and onion thickened with maize dough, *indio viejo* (old Indian) is another Nicaraguan dish that has its roots in pre-Columbian times. According to legend, a group of hungry Spanish conquistadors arrived in an indigenous village demanding to know what the locals were cooking. "Only an old Indian who died yesterday," a quick-witted member of the tribe responded. The ruse worked. Shocked at this story of cannibalism, the

Spaniards rode off to raid another village, and the whole tribe had a good laugh as they enjoyed the meal of maize that had been cooking over the fire. *Indio viejo* gets its slightly sweet flavor from *yerba buena* and bitter orange, and is traditionally served with *tostones* (fried green plantains) and *cuajada* (curd cheese).

Rondón: a classic of Creole cooking on the Atlantic coast of Nicaragua, *rondón* is a one-pot cooking solution for busy fishermen that has become an iconic dish for the whole region. Fish, shrimp, lobster, or any other seafood are added to the pot with root vegetables such as *yuca*, potatoes, and carrots, with bell peppers, chilis, and a fish stock sweetened with coconut milk. *Rondón* can also be made with beef, pork, or turtle meat, but the creamy coconut works best with seafood.

Sweet Treats

Nicaraguans don't generally have a sweet dish after a main meal in a restaurant, but there are a few options for those seeking a sugar fix.

Buñuelos: a street-food staple made from *yuca* flour, mixed with eggs and cheese and deep-fried to create crunchy balls of joy. Hot syrup flavored with cinnamon is poured over them to give a warm, ticky sweetness to the salty savoriness of the cheesy *yuca* balls.

Güirilas: slightly sweet, slightly salty, and delicious when combined with homemade *cuajada* and cream, the *güirila* (corn pancake) is one of the gastronomic delights of the Nicaraguan countryside. The spelling can put off some visitors, but just ask for a "wee-ri-la."

Flan: a Nicaraguan version of cream caramel, a cold egg custard topped with caramel sauce

Tres leches: a delicious combination of sponge cake soaked in milk, condensed milk, and layered in cream.

Cajetas: homemade candies that run the gamut from sticky toffees made from condensed milk to coconut fancies in radioactive shades of fuchsia

Rosquillas: hard biscuits in the shape of a ring—firm local favorites, combining *cuajada*, maize dough, butter, and milk

Fritangas

When it comes to eating out, the first choice for most Nicaraguans is their neighborhood *fritanga*, a roadside barbecue where meat is cooked over hot coals and served up with a hefty side of rice and beans, crispy plantains, and a cold drink. A source of great local pride, *fritangas* are an integral part of Nicaragua's gastronomic identity. The popular cumbia-rock band La Cuneta Son Machin even wrote an ode, "Amor Fritanguero" (Fritanga Love) to the Nicaraguan love of sizzling street meat. Options at a *fritanga* include:

Asado: Barbecued *pollo* (chicken), *cerdo* (pork), *carne de res* (beef), or *costillas* (ribs)

Chorizo: Spicy sausage

Enchiladas: Tortillas stuffed with rice and beef, folded in half, battered, and deep fried

Maduro: Whole ripe plantain, sometimes served *con queso* (with cheese)

Manuelitas: Rolled pancakes filled with cheese sweetened with sugar and cinnamon

Moronga: Blood sausage

Tacos: Deep fried tortilla tubes filled with beef

Tajadas: Thin, crispy slices of fried plantain

Tortepapa: A battered potato cake filled with cheese

Vegetarians and Vegans

With staples like *frijoles rojos* (red beans), *arroz* (rice), *cuajada*, *yuca* (cassava), and *plátanos* (plantains) in all their varieties and maize tortillas available everywhere, vegetarians will have no problem with eating in Nicaragua. Pescatarians will find an abundance of fish and seafood along the Pacific and Atlantic coasts, and fruitarians will love the dizzying range of familiar and less familiar tropical fruits sold whole or as juices on street stalls and in markets.

Vegans, however, will need to be creative when negotiating menus. Outside the tourist-friendly towns, where it's fairly easy to find vegan menu options, there is no widespread understanding of what it actually means to be a *vegano* (vay-ga-no).

Always take care when ordering food. If you ask for a dish *sin carne*, this means "without red meat," not "without meat," so your choice could still contain chicken, pork, sausages, or even black pudding. Also bear in mind that vegetable soups are often made with meat stock, and beans are often cooked with *manteca* (pork lard). Luckily, the natural willingness of Nicaraguans to accommodate guests means that cooks when asked are usually happy to make an omelet, or add extra *platanos* or avocado to jazz up a porkless plate of rice and beans. The secret, as always, is to master the Spanish words you need to request alternatives.

Some hostels have kitchens where guests can cook their own meals with supplies from the local market.

DRINKS
Refrescos—Cold Drinks
Nicaragua's semi-tropical climate and diverse ecology zones make it the perfect place to cultivate a colorful array of fruits from which to squeeze or blend *jugos* (juices). There are familiar fruits like *naranja* (orange), *piña* (pineapple), *sandía* (watermelon), *tamarindo*

(tamarind), papaya, and mango, and the more exotic *calala* (passionfruit), *guayaba* (guava), and *guanabana* (soursop). Popular local fruits that visitors should try include *jocote* (which is also eaten with salt), *mamón* (mamoncillo), *nancite* (nance), *níspero* (sapodilla), pitaya (dragon fruit), and the small, dark berries of the *coyolito* (corozo fruit).

TIPPING

There is no formal requirement to tip in Nicaragua. In restaurants a 10 percent service charge is often already incorporated into the bill, but you can ask for it to be removed if you don't feel the service was adequate. A 10 percent tip for the server is otherwise up to you, but will definitely be well received.

Many people live from the tips they receive, and everyone, from the hotel doorman to car park attendants and wandering musicians, will expect a tip. As in restaurants, this is at your discretion.

For tour guides, calculate a tip of around $10 per person, but it depends on the size of your group and how happy you are with the tour. You should also consider a (smaller) tip for the driver.

With taxis there are no meters, so you need to negotiate the fare before you get in. Nicaraguans don't tip taxi drivers, but if you get a tour with your ride and help with heavy suitcases you might want to add a few dollars on top of the fare.

Nicaraguans also make a sweet, purple *chicha de maíz* (maize mixed with water and sugar) drink and all manner of cold chocolate drinks from ground *cacao* (cocoa), which is mixed with ground toasted maize to make *tiste,* or *pinolillo* (when cinnamon and pepper are added), or *tibio* (when served hot). To offset the slight grittiness of the roughly ground maize and cocoa, drinkers swirl the cup around, so much so that swirling drinks is considered a national trait.

A Puro Pinolero

The local love of *pinolillo* has given rise to the name *pinolero* to describe a Nicaraguan who is proud of his roots. It also prompted the patriotic phrase, *Soy puro Pinolero! Nicaragüense por gracias de Dios!* (I am pure Pinolero! Nicaraguan thanks to God!), which comes from the famous song "Nicaragua Mía" composed by Tino Lopez Guerra.

Ground maize, rice, *jicaro* seeds, chia seeds, *cebada* (barley) and *avena* (oatmeal) are also mixed with water or milk and sweetened to make a range of different drinks. Just like fruit juices, these drinks come under the category *frescos,* which shouldn't be confused with the *refrescos* (fizzy sodas) of other Spanish-speaking countries. In Nicaragua fizzy sodas are called *gaseosas.*

Fritangas, comedores, and street stalls known as *refrescarías* all sell *frescos,* most often in a plastic bag with ice and a straw. It can seem strange at first to drink from a bag, but you'll soon get the hang of it— though don't fiddle with the knot at the top of the bag!

There are several local and US *gaseosas* (sodas) available, but Nicaraguans will almost always refer to any dark cola as *una negra* (a black one) and cherryade as *una rojita* (a little red one).

Hot Drinks

The northern highlands of Jinotega, Matagalpa, and Nueva Segovia produce some of the best shade-grown, high-altitude arabica coffee in the world in and on the fertile slopes of the country's many volcanoes, so there is a great variety of coffees to try. Some of the best beans are exported, but even at roadside stalls the strong, black *café negro* is generally good, and connoisseurs will easily find the beans for sale in supermarkets, and directly from the growers if you visit a coffee hacienda or cooperative farm.

Nicaraguans favor cheap and cheerful coffees like Presto, an instant coffee produced for the local market. For real ground coffee on a budget try Café Toro, which packs a punch, and for top-quality beans seek out San Sebastian, La Iguana, or Las Flores. *Café con leche* is coffee with milk. *Café negro* is black.

The most interesting way to learn about Nicaraguan coffee is to buy it direct from the farm and enjoy a tour. German farmers were the first to bring coffee to Nicaragua in the nineteenth century, and that tradition survives at the Selva Negra Hacienda near Matagalpa, which has pioneered sustainable and organic production methods. At the famous Hacienda Las Flores, on the slopes of the Mombacho volcano near Granada, you can learn about coffee production, try a variety of premium brews, and then go ziplining through the canopy. Many small cooperatives also run coffee operations that rely on Fairtrade initiatives and appreciate visits.

Tea is generally weak and watery, US style. Herbal teas like *manzanilla* (chamomile) are fairly common in hotels and hostels, but out in rural areas most Nicaraguans are fueled by coffee.

Alcoholic Drinks

Nicaraguans are beer (*cerveza*) and rum (*ron*) drinkers. They favor a golden, pilsner-style beer, drunk very cold and at any time of day. Toña (4.6 percent) is the best- selling beer, and you will see billboards all over the country carrying its catchy slogan, *Como mi Toña ninguna!* (There's nothing like my Toña). Its slightly stronger (4.9 percent) rival, Victoria, is actually produced by the same brewery, the Compañía Cervecera de Nicaragua, which also produces Light and Frost versions of the beers.

The fashion for craft beers and microbreweries has seen local start-ups, such as Moropotente, do well with IPAs and stouts, and there is a craft beer bar in San Juan del Sur. The Compañía Cervecera de Nicaragua has even launched its own craft-style brand, Mytos. You can get some imported foreign beers in bars and clubs in Managua, Granada, and San Juan del Sur— but why, when the local beers are so good?

When it comes to rum, the Nicaraguans are blessed with one of the best in the world. Flor de Caña is excellent quality and reasonably priced, starting at around US $10 for a four- or five-year-old, slow-aged Añejo Clasico. The most popular seller is the seven-year-old Gran Reserva, but they also sell a twelve-year-old Centenario, and ultra-premium eighteen- and twenty-five-year-old versions. A popular day trip from León is the Flor de Caña factory tour in Chichigalpa, where you can see the bourbon barrels used in the ageing process, visit the storehouses, and try a thirty-year-old rum from the barrel. The owner of Flor de Caña is Carlos Pellas, the richest man in Nicaragua. His family started the San Antonio sugar plantation in 1890, and they now make other brands of rum, such as Ron Plata. During the violence and uncertainty of the Contra War in the 1980s the company placed a large quantity of its rum barrels in protective storage so that today it boasts one of the largest reserves of aged rum in the world.

At the low end of local liquor production are the plastic bottles of cheap, industrially produced *aguardiente* (firewater), like Caballito (Little Horse), Joyita (Little Jewel), and Estrellita (Little Star), which are best drunk in fruit cocktails.

COCKTAIL TIME

In 2006 a group of local tour operators, the tourism board INTUR, and Flor de Caña held a competition to choose a national drink. The result was the Macuá, a refreshing mix of white rum, guava juice, orange juice, lemon juice, and syrup, served in a tall glass over ice. Named after a local bird, the swallow-tailed swift *Panyptila cayennensis*, the Macuá was dreamed up by Dr. Edmundo Miranda, a pediatrician from Granada.

Homemade moonshine distilled from maize and known as *guaro, lija,* or *cususa,* can vary in quality. At Christmas and festivals, especially in the northern hills, they still produce a fermented alcohol drink made from maize known as *chicha bruja,* which was the indigenous beer used before the arrival of the Spanish. The Garifuna communities of Laguna de Perla have their own hooch called *gifiti* or *guiffity*, a homemade concoction of *aguardiente* or rum mixed with medicinal roots, herbs, and garlic that is left to marinade for weeks or months. The Garifuna rave about its health-giving properties, especially its powerful aphrodisiac effects, but all such drinks are best approached with caution.

THE ARTS

Nicaragua has a rich culture of folk songs, masked folk dances, and handicrafts, but it can also boast painters of international renown such as Armando Morales, a strong history of literature and poetry that includes the father of Latin American *modernismo*, Rubén Darío, a vibrant music scene that has gone from patriotic protest songs to modern party anthems, and a fledgling film industry making movies on contemporary social issues.

Music and Dance

The soundtrack to life in Nicaragua is always there in the background: the rata-tat-tat of the school marching drums, the plinkety-plonk of the marimba, the rousing revolutionary ballads extolling the unparalleled virtues of the land and people, the twerky reggaeton on the

radio, the salsa on the bus, the mariachi music of Mexico in the bar on the corner, the brass-band blare of the *chicheros* animating a street parade, and the cumbia that gets everybody to their feet at a *fiesta*.

At national celebrations or folk-dance events the instrument you are most likely to hear is the marimba, a New World cousin of the African belafon. All marimbas are made of wooden keys struck with mallets to produce their distinctive sound, but the Nicaraguan marimba is unique as it is played sitting down. Popular songs like "Solar de Monimbó" and "La Mora Limpia" are usually played on marimba, guitar, and *guitarilla*.

In the 1970s the influence of Cuban *nova trova* saw the emergence of a new brand of socially aware folk singers such as Carlos and Luis Enrique Mejía Godoy from Somoto, and groups like Duo Guardabarranco. Carlos Mejía Godoy's "Nicaragua Nicaraguita" is a love song to the country that's become an alternative anthem.

In the northern uplands, the European settlers who came to grow coffee in the nineteenth century brought with them a tradition of polkas, mazurkas, waltzes, and *jamaquellos* played on guitar, mandolin, violin, and accordion. This *música norteña*, popularized by Don Felipe Urrutia and Ulises González, can still be heard at local *fiestas*.

On the Atlantic coast, with its English and Afro-Caribbean influences, groups like Dimension Costeña play percussive dance music with the soca and calypso rhythms popular at the Palo de Mayo festival.

A new wave of Nicaraguan rock bands is led by La Cuneta Son Machin, who play an infectious mix of cumbia and rock and are the first Nicaraguan band nominated for a Grammy Award. The Cuneta tell stories about Nicaraguan daily life much like the folk singers who came before them but with an irreverent humor that revels in Nica-speak.

A Nicaraguan artist who has won a Grammy Award is the salsa singer Luis Enrique, who was a leading light of the *salsa romántica* scene in the 1990s.

Cinema

There are several Hollywood movies about Nicaragua. The most bizarre must be *Walker* (1987), Alex Cox's unconventional retelling of William Walker's failed attempt to take over Nicaragua in the 1860s, starring Ed Harris as the villainous Walker. Cox tries to draw parallels between Walker's destructive Central American exploits and the aggressive interventionist policies of the USA under Ronald Reagan in the 1980s.

More successful is *Carla's Song* (1997), by British director Ken Loach, which follows a Scottish bus driver who is sucked into the Contra War in Estelí after falling in love with a Nicaraguan refugee in Glasgow.

Two films about journalists caught up in intrigues in Nicaragua are noteworthy: *Under Fire* (1983), which sees Nick Nolte in the thick of a fictionalized Sandinista uprising; and *Shoot the Messenger* (2014), which delves into the web of deceit uncovered by investigative journalist Gary Webb as he tried to piece together the links between the CIA, US-backed Contra rebels, and the drugs flooding poor neighborhoods in the USA.

Nicaragua's first home-grown feature film is *La Yuma* (2010) by the French-born director Florence Jaugey. It tells the tale of a young girl from a poor background who starts boxing to break out of the macho world that surrounds her. Jaugey's follow-up, *La Pantalla Desnuda* (The Naked Screen, 2014), explores the problem of revenge porn in a switched-on social media world after a girl allows her boyfriend to film them on his phone.

Visual Arts

The earliest examples of Nicaragua's colorful pre-Columbian ceramics and stone sculptures, some showing Mayan and later Aztec influence, can be found in the Palacio de la Cultura, the former National Assembly in Managua. The Chorotega people carved monumental stone sculptures depicting anthropomorphic figures or priests in animal disguises at a ceremonial center in Isla Zapatera, and these can be seen at the Convento San Francisco in Granada. Examples of Spanish-style colonial art can be found in churches and museums around the country.

Muralism became very popular in the mid-1960s and '70s, particularly in opposition to the Somoza dictatorship. Most of the most famous Sandinista murals of revolutionary martyrs that adorned the streets of Managua have been painted over, but you can still find some good examples in Estelí and León. In the 1950s the painter Rodrigo Peñalba was an influential figure who taught and inspired many of the artists who belonged to the 1960s Praxis group, such as the painter and muralist Leóncio Sáenz, who explored themes of national identity and Nicaragua's indigenous past.

A *primitivista* or naive art style was fostered by the priest, poet, and left-wing politician Ernesto Cardenal on the islands of the Solentiname archipelago with the help of painter Róger Pérez de la Rocha. The Rubén Darío Teatro Nacional has a good display of modern paintings and sculptures by national artists, but the Museo de Arte Fundación Ortiz-Gurdián in León has the most extensive collection of modern and contemporary art in the country. Housed in two colonial *quintas*, the Ortiz-Gurdián is considered one of the best art museums in Central America and shows works by international artists such as Picasso, Chagall, and Miró. A highlight of the museum is a series of lithographs featuring the national hero General Augusto Sandino by Armando Morales, Nicaragua's most internationally renowned painter.

Literature and Books
Dubbed "The Land of Poets," Nicaragua can boast the most toasted lyrical maestro of his generation, Rubén Darío (1867–1916), the father of Spanish modernism, a literary rebellion that helped the writers of Latin America break free from the shackles of Spanish colonial convention. His most influential book, *Azul* (Blue), was published in 1888 and quickly established his international reputation. Working as a journalist and diplomat, Darío traveled widely in Central and South America, Spain, and France, leading the life of a poet in Paris, where he was influenced by the Symbolists and Paul Verlaine. His bohemian lifestyle took its toll, however, and on February 6, 1916, the Prince of Castilian Letters died in León. The writer Sergio Ramírez, a former vice-president in the Sandinista government of Daniel Ortega, has explored the life and legacy of Rubén Darío.

Ramírez' novels deal with important chapters in Nicaragua's history and have been widely translated. In 2017 he won the Cervantes Prize, the most prestigious literary honor in the Spanish-speaking world, for his books *Margarita, How Beautiful the Sea,* and *Adiós Muchachos: A Memoir of the Sandinista Revolution.* Most books about Nicaragua written by foreign writers focus on the Somoza years, the Sandinista uprising, and the Contra wars. Salman Rushdie's *Jaguar Smile* (1988), a slim volume recounting a brief visit to the country under the Sandinistas, is best read in conjunction with local poet and novelist Gioconda Belli's passionate biographical account of the revolutionary years, *The Country Under My Skin.* (See page 165.)

SPORTS AND OUTDOOR ACTIVITIES

Futbol (soccer) may be king in most of Central America, but here *beisbol* (baseball) is the most popular sport by a mile. Boxing is a religion. Outdoor sports such as hiking up volcanoes, kayaking in the two huge freshwater lakes, and sea and river fishing are all popular, but the biggest weekend crowds are drawn to surfing the perfect breakers of the Pacific.

Play Ball

Baseball arrived in Nicaragua in the 1880s, when US businessman Albert Addlesberg convinced the Creole-speaking boys of Bluefields to lay down their cricket bats and take up a new game. Baseball fever soon spread, and in 1891 the first big game was played between Managua and Granada. The arrival of US Marines in 1912 further helped to cement the sport's position as the national game. The four main teams are Indios del Bóer, Leónes de León, Tigres del Chinandega, and Orientales de Granada.

Nicaragua's greatest baseball hero is the pitcher Dennis Martínez, who in 1976 became the first Nicaraguan to play in the US Major Leagues when he joined the Baltimore Orioles. Born in Granada, Martínez achieved 245 major-league wins in his twenty-three-year career, and earned the nickname "El Presidente" from US fans, although in Nicaragua he is known as "El Chirizo," which refers to his thick hair. In 1991 he became the thirteenth pitcher to throw a perfect game in the US, and the first from Latin America. When a 15,000-capacity baseball stadium was opened in Managua in 2017 it was named Estadio Nacional Dennis Martínez in his honor.

Local baseball games are well worth attending, even if just for the atmosphere as you mingle with the Nicaraguan spectators.

The Noble Art of Knock Outs

Nicaragua's greatest boxing legend is Alexis Arguello, "El Flaco Explosive" (The Explosive Thin Man), a gifted and powerful puncher who between 1974 and 1982 won championship titles at three weight divisions: featherweight, junior lightweight, and lightweight. After boxing he turned to politics and was elected Mayor of Managua in 2008, but was tragically found dead in 2009. Arguello helped to train Roman González, "Chocolatito", a boy who went from collecting garbage in a horse and cart with his father in Managua to world championships at four weight divisions: super flyweight, flyweight, light flyweight, and strawweight. González' unbeaten run of forty-six fights ended in 2017.

Another famous fighter is the showman Ricardo Mayorga, "El Matador," whose exploits earned him the title of "The Craziest Man in Boxing."

Local boys often face off in a makeshift ring before a rodeo or *fiesta*.

Soccer

Internationally, Nicaragua has never been a great soccer nation, but that doesn't mean Nicaraguans aren't glued to the screen when the national side takes to the field. Given how many kids you see kicking soccer balls around in dusty fields after school, it's surprising that the sport hasn't taken off. There are ten teams in the top Primera Division, including top teams Real Estelí from Estelí, Deportivo Walter Ferretti and Juventus from Managua, and Diriangén from Diriamba, one of the oldest soccer clubs in Central America.

Rural Sports

In rural areas, *corridas* (bullfights) or *barreras de toros* (bull-riding rodeos) are hugely popular, especially during the *fiestas* for local saints, but unlike the choreographed slaughter of Spanish bullfights, in Nicaragua the bulls are not killed. Young men test their courage by stepping into the ring with the bulls, or see how long they can stay on a bucking bull.

You can find a *pelea de gallo* (cockfight) in most towns and villages, typically in a *gallera* (cockfighting ring) where both men and women bet on the bloody battles between the fighting roosters fitted with sharpened metal spurs.

Surfing the Waves

The Pacific coast of Nicaragua is world famous for its year-round surf, with big waves in the rainy season and smaller waves in the dry season. The country's surfing capital is San Juan del Sur, a former fishing village on a wide crescent bay that has become Nicaragua's number-one party town and an expat magnet without completely losing its charm. Surf schools here take advantage of the year-round waves at nearby beaches like Playa Remanso, perfect for learners, and Playa Maderas, for all levels. Intermediate and professional surfers head north to Popoyo, and those seeking big waves continue on to the point at El Astillero.

For an upmarket surfing experience there are several surf camps operating on more remote stretches of the coast, where yoga and wellness treatments are usually included with surf lessons. Or follow the Hollywood A-listers south to Nicaragua's most luxurious resort, Mukul, owned by the Flor de Caña rum magnate Don Carlos Pellas. There's also an eighteen-hole golf course there, with spectacular sea views.

chapter seven

TRAVEL, HEALTH, & SAFETY

Nicaragua is one of the largest countries in Central America. It has a good transportation infrastructure along the Pacific side and through the central region, where the majority of its six million inhabitants live. Traveling by public transportation, taxi, or tour bus is cheaper than in North America or Europe, easy to organize, and relatively safe. Nicaraguans are friendly travel companions and will easily strike up a conversation on a bus or try to give travel tips even if communication is limited by the language barrier.

Until recently the country was sometimes divided in two in the rainy season, when heavy downpours and swollen rivers washed out the roads that linked the developed cities and towns of the Pacific coast with the more isolated communities along the wild shores of the Mosquito Coast. That situation is changing fast, opening up the whole country to greater integration, commerce, and tourism.

One of the joys of traveling in Nicaragua is to take a bus or taxi along a modern highway to arrive at a place where the next leg of your trip may be on a horse and carriage through the cobbled streets of a colonial village, or on a *panga*—a motorized boat taxi—for a three-hour journey along a jungle-bordered river. The more remote the region you visit, the more rustic the transportation becomes, and the more interesting the adventure.

Nicaragua is consistently rated the safest country in the region—a huge achievement, given the problems experienced by its neighbors to the north—but you should still take all sensible precautions to avoid being the victim of petty crime when traveling on public transportation, or while waiting at bus stations.

BY AIR

The main airport is the Aeropuerto Internacional Augusto C. Sandino, on the outskirts of Managua. There are direct flights from Miami, Houston, Dallas, Atlanta, and Fort Lauderdale in the US, with more flights expected from other US cities as tourism numbers grow. Canadian and European travelers still have to transfer through a US or Central American hub.

Have some cash handy when you arrive, as all tourists and business travelers entering the country by air currently have to pay US $10 at passport control. No visa is needed when entering by air, and tourists are issued with a thirty-day tourist card that can be extended in Managua up to ninety days.

Internal Flights

Taking an internal flight is the fastest and most comfortable way to travel from Managua to destinations on the Atlantic coast, or to the popular Caribbean destination of Big Corn Island. Aerotaxis La Costeña, based at the International Airport in Managua, is the only local carrier operating scheduled routes. It flies to Bilwi, Bluefields, San Juan de Nicaragua, San Carlos, Ometepe, the towns of the mining triangle, Big Corn Island, and Tegucigalpa in Honduras.

Travelers should bear in mind that planes are small and flights are often fully booked. Make arrangements well in advance, and be at the airport two hours before departure. There are strict limits on checked luggage, and bulky items may be refused. There is also a US $2 departure tax on internal flights. It is highly advisable to reconfirm your return trip immediately upon arrival at your destination, rather than waiting till your departure. Local airstrips can be extremely basic, especially in the mining triangle of Siuna, Rosita, and Bonanza (where the airport terminal is dwarfed by the next-door bar).

Some luxury hotels and resorts offer their guests transport in private planes and helicopters, like the exclusive Mukul Beach, Spa and Golf Resort, which has its own air transport from Managua to the airport on the Emerald Coast.

ON THE ROADS

In Managua the number of cars, taxis, and buses on the roads leads to gridlock at peak hours, and you should take a taxi during the day if you need to be anywhere fast, and at night for safety. The capital also has a mind-boggling address system based on landmarks as reference points (see opposite) that can make driving yourself from place to place feel like a patience-sapping exercise in futility. Taxis are cheap and plentiful, so take advantage of those until you get your bearings.

The main road that runs through the country is the famous Pan-American Highway, known in Central America as the Inter-American Highway. From Honduras it passes through Ocotal, Estelí, and Managua, and continues on to Jinotepe and Rivas, where it runs parallel to Lago de Cocibolca (Lake Nicaragua) before reaching Costa Rica at Peñas Blancas.

MANAGUA: WHERE THE STREETS HAVE NO NAMES

Nicaraguans will tell you that it was after visiting Managua in 1986 that Bono wrote U2's famous song "Where the Streets Have No Name." Try to orient yourself in the sprawling capital, and you will soon see why. Rather than street addresses, Nicaraguans navigate by landmarks, which is not too confusing if you can find them—but many no longer exist. Some were destroyed in the earthquake that flattened the old city center in 1972, and others are so ancient that they exist only in the collective unconscious. The result is that addresses sound more like little poems than practical instructions. Directions might start with: "*donde fue el Hospital Militar, una cuadra al lago, tres cuadras abajo, 50 metros al sur,*" or "where the Military Hospital used to be, one block to the lake, three blocks east, fifty meters south." The use of Lake Managua as a reference point is particularly frustrating if you are stuck in traffic with no idea of where it might be. To add to the surreal poetry, *arriba* (up) is used to indicate west, and *abajo* (down) to indicate east, which can result in the bizarre experience of going "down" while traveling uphill.

Una cuadra is a city block, but Nicaraguans often refer to one as *una manzana*, which has nothing to do with an apple but is a land measurement equal to 1.74 acres. Also, instead of miles or meters, you might be given distances in *varas*, an antiquated measurement roughly equivalent to a yard. The same address system applies all over the country. But while narrow colonial streets and one-way traffic systems may lead you on a merry dance around Masaya, León, and Matagalpa, Managua is most likely to drive you loopy.

Road quality is generally improving, accompanied by clearer signposting and markings, but even important roads like the Pan-American Highway only have one lane in each direction, with a few multi-lane sections round cities. In the past, bad roads combined with bad weather meant that communication between the Pacific and the autonomous Atlantic regions was sometimes cut off in the rainy season, but new paved roads now allow faster and more reliable access to Bilwi (Puerto Cabezas), and Bluefields. Elsewhere in the countryside, dirt roads can still become impassable after heavy rain and even Managua's streets can be affected by downpours, slowing traffic across the city. A major drive to improve rural roads is helping to reduce journey times in the countryside, and a new coastal highway linking the surf beaches and resorts of the Pacific coast to the border with Costa Rica is expected to encourage more tourism development in the region.

Taxis

Low prices mean taxis are a great way to travel in Nicaraguan cities, especially after dark, or when traveling to places where security is an issue. Official taxis have red license plates with a white border, unlike private cars, which have white plates. For security it is best to avoid unlicensed taxis, known as *piratas* (pirates). At night, it is always safer to have your hotel or a restaurant call you a taxi than to hail one on the street.

There are no meters, so agree a price before getting in. Short rides within most towns and cities outside Managua can cost less than US $1, but at Managua airport and outside hotels the taxis at the stands will generally quote higher prices than taxis flagged down in the street. Foreign visitors can expect to be quoted the "*chele*" price by drivers, so ask at your hotel or hostel how much they would themselves expect to pay, be prepared to haggle, and maybe let a few go before you can negotiate a better fare.

Most taxis operate as *colectivos*, meaning they will stop for other passengers en route, which can be a disconcerting experience for first-time visitors. Specify that you want to go "*directo, no colectivo*" and for a higher price they will take you straight there.

Colorful Local Transportation

Few cities in Nicaragua outside Managua have formal bus services, and many people rely on *colectivos* (taxis and mini-vans), and *caponeras* (bicycle or motorbike taxis) to get to school and work.

Once upon a time, the horse and buggy was the main local transportation option, and the tradition survives in some places. In Granada, you have rather grand carriages painted in bright colors to attract tourists for clip-clopping tours around the cobbled streets, but in nearby Masaya you can still find the locals taking home the groceries in a horse and buggy. Elsewhere, the *caponera* is king. *Caponeras* are either three-wheeled bicycle taxis with the driver at the back and passengers

on a seat in front covered by a fabric roof, or motorbike taxis, usually painted red, that zip around fast like angry hornets. There are also hybrids, with a bicycle taxi seat in front and a motorbike behind. Bus stations and road intersections are usually thick with *caponeras* waiting for clients. They are cheap, and prices are fixed so locals don't even ask the fare when they jump in. To avoid being charged a tourist price, always ask locals for prices and confirm with the driver before setting off.

In some places, such as San Juan del Sur, there is a shuttle service in adapted *camionetas* (pickup trucks) to the surf beaches of Marsella, Maderas, and Masagual, but generally beware of traveling in open-top trucks on Nicaraguan roads. A taxi is a safer option.

Buses

Apart from the luxury buses that travel between countries in Central America, and the private coaches ferrying tourists around, you can forget air-conditioned comfort, reclining seats, and on-board movies. Most buses in Nicaragua are reconditioned Blue Bird school buses from the USA, and are known as "chicken buses," because either the passengers are crowded in like chickens or they are carrying chickens with them. Some are still painted the standard school-bus yellow, but the majority have been primped out by their proud owners with loud paint jobs in carnival colors and even louder sound systems to animate long journeys. With luggage stashed on the roof, these go-anywhere buses travel up and down the country over potholes and up steep hills to the remotest destinations. Expect bruised knees in seats originally designed for pre-teens, and plenty of opportunities to get up close and personal with your fellow passengers as more people cram themselves in at every stop. The chicken bus experience is rarely dull.

At bus stations and at stops along the route, hawkers swarm aboard to sell sodas and street food. Out of nowhere, a preacher might stand up and start quoting the Bible, keen to bring the good word.

In Managua there are four bus stations: the Mercado El Mayoreo, Mercado Israel Lewites, and Mercado Roberto Huembes are all at markets; the bus station at the Universidad Centroamericana (UCA, pronounced Ooh-Ka) is the place to get a minibus to Masaya and Granada. Some towns may have two bus stations, and smaller towns and villages may just have a place on the road where people wait for a bus. Always ask and double check where buses leave from and at what times, to avoid getting stranded. For road safety reasons it is always better to travel in the daytime.

Car Rental

If you plan to drive yourself around Nicaragua, a number of international and local car rental firms operate at Managua Airport, at the border with Costa Rica, and in the main cities. Generally, you need to be at least twenty-five years of age to rent a car, although some companies can arrange more expensive deals for younger drivers over twenty-one. A valid driver's license is essential, either from your own country or an international license, and you must pay with a credit card. Read the contract carefully and factor in any extra taxes and insurance costs. Always check the brakes, seatbelts, and tires, and make sure there is a working car-jack (*gato*) and spare tire (*llanta de repuesto*). Note any dents or problems and sign them off with the rental agency before taking the car out, and take a few photographs to avoid any arguments later.

Renting a car gives you the freedom to explore at your own pace, but with taxis so cheap and driving conditions different from those at home, you may find it works out more easily and cheaply to take taxis or pay a local driver to take you out on day trips. This can also avoid any problems if you have an accident, as Nicaraguan road rules are strict, and drivers can have their identity documents withheld, or be detained by the police until responsibility for a crash is determined.

Rules of the Road

Nicaraguans drive on the right, as they do in the USA, and the rules are similar. Drivers and front-seat passengers must wear seat belts, and drivers must be able to produce a valid license and the documents of the car when challenged by a *policía de tránsito* (traffic cop).

Speed limits vary from 45 kmph (28 mph) in towns and cities, 60 kmph (37 mph) on highways, and 100 kmph (62 mph) on freeways, but drivers must be eagle-eyed for road signs that show a sudden change in the speed limit on stretches of road that pass a school.

In Managua drivers have to be both aggressive, to make progress in traffic, and defensive, as other drivers swerve around and cut in front of each other. You also have to be aware of taxis, motorbikes, buses, and even horses pulling carts, jostling for space. Outside the cities, the biggest dangers on Nicaraguan roads are wandering livestock, cows, oxen, and horses, and bicycles without lights.

Traffic cops can give an on-the-spot fine for infractions like overtaking where there's an unbroken white line on the road, or for speeding. The driver's documents are held until the fine is paid at a bank. In the event of an accident where somebody is injured or killed, drivers can be held in jail and their identity papers and passport retained until liability and damage claims are settled.

Fuel

Gas is sold by the liter, and there are three types available: regular, super, and diesel. Gas is pumped by an attendant, and Nicaraguans do not generally tip unless the attendant checks the air or cleans the windshield as well. Gas sells for around a dollar a liter, but fill up where you can, as service stations are harder to find as you get deeper into the countryside.

BY BOAT

With two of the largest lakes in Central America, and major rivers demarcating part of the northern border with Honduras and the southern border with Costa Rica, ferries and *pangas* (boat taxis) are the only way to visit some destinations.

The port of San Jorge, near Rivas, is the departure point for the car ferries that travel to the twin-volcano island of Ometepe in the Lago Cocibolca (Lake Nicaragua). Cars go below and passengers sit up on the deck for the sometimes choppy crossing to the town of Moyogalpa, which takes about an hour, depending on conditions.

Pangas are the only public transportation along the Río San Juan, which snakes its way from San Carlos on Lake Nicaragua down past the rapids at El Castillo to San Juan de Nicaragua on the Atlantic coast. San Carlos is also the place to get a boat out to the Solentiname archipelago, famous for its primitivist painters.

Along the Mosquito Coast, open-top *pangas* are the main transport connecting Bilwi with Miskito and Creole villages, while from Bluefields *pangas* travel to Laguna de Perlas and on to remote Garifuna communities like Orinoco. From Big Corn Island to Little Corn Island, the thirty-minute boat trip in an uncovered *panga* can be quite an adventure if you run into a squall.

The main port at Corinto on the Pacific coast is seeing a growing number of cruise ship arrivals, and improvements at the port of San Juan del Sur have made it possible for larger cruise ships to dock.

WHERE TO STAY

Nicaragua was considered a hardship posting back in the dark days of the Contra War and the difficult economic times that followed it, but things have changed dramatically and tourism is booming, with new hostels, hotels, and luxury resorts springing up all over the country. In Managua you can find comfortable and modern five-, four-, and three-star hotels aimed at business travelers and foreign tourists run by a range of international chains, including Hilton, Hyatt, Intercontinental, Holiday Inn, and Best Western.

In Granada, the main destination for foreign tourists, the central plaza is ringed by colonial mansions from the city's glory days that have been converted into top-end hotels, with some offering coveted views of the cathedral. Elsewhere in the city, new boutique options have opened their doors, like the Hotel Real de La Merced, a restored mansion that boasts a staircase made of pink marble shipped over from Italy in the 1930s and the city's first swimming pool. Out on Las Isletas, luxury wellness spas have sprung up. Jicaro Island Lodge, a little oasis of luxury and pampering, has played host to Hollywood A-listers.

In León, a restored convent, El Convento, has cool, cloistered rooms offering respite from the heat outside, and corridors packed with antique altars and icons.

Along the Pacific coast, funky surf hangouts with yoga decks and vegan menu options jostle for space with cheap and cheerful backpacker hostels.

Offering a new level of luxury, the Mukul Beach, Golf and Spa resort occupies an unspoiled stretch along the Emerald Coast. The brainchild of the Flor de Caña rum magnate Carlos Pellas, it offers guests an exclusive beach experience, with surf lessons, yoga classes, helicopter trips, and the opportunity to play eighteen holes of golf on a course designed by British architect David McLay Kidd.

At the other end of the scale, in the Miraflor Natural Reserve in the northern hills above Estelí, you can share the humble wooden shack of a local family on a home-stay program, and learn more about the lives of these small, coffee-growing communities. Such home-stays offer a cheap, stimulating, and sometimes challenging option for those seeking to immerse themselves in the language and culture of the country, and are excellent ways to meet and make friends with Nicaraguans.

On the Atlantic coast, you can stay in traditional stilt houses built over the water in Pearl Lagoon, or string up a hammock under the stars on the Pearl Cays. On Little Corn Island you can go to the other extreme at the

Yemaya Island Hideaway and Spa, where the coddled customers want for nothing on their private stretch of paradise, and the bamboo beach bar serves up potent coco-loco cocktails.

Prices for accommodation increase during the *temporada alta* (high season), which includes Christmas, New Year, Carnival, and Easter. During these periods, rooms at beach resorts or in cities and towns with popular local festivals should be booked well in advance. The low season at the end of September through October is a good time to look for discounts.

HEALTH

There are no compulsory vaccinations for visiting Nicaragua, but see "Vaccinations" on page 132, and have the necessary jabs before you travel. Prevention is better than cure, so take sensible measures such as drinking bottled water and skipping leafy salads. The sun can be fierce, especially when you climb a volcano at midday, but even on cloudy days you can get burnt, so apply sunscreen, wear a hat, and rehydrate regularly. In forest areas, mosquitoes come out to bite as the sun sets, so pack long-sleeved shirts and long pants, and slap on the bug repellent before they get you.

The Health System

There is a two-tier health system in Nicaragua: a public health service that is free to all, provided by the state, and a private system. There have been major investments in the public health system in the last few years, with more local clinics and hospitals being built in rural areas and the introduction of *casas maternas*, which look after pregnant women just before they are due to give birth.

A *centro de salud* (public health center) can deal with most minor ailments and accidents, or the local *farmacía* (drugstore) is another option. Many medicines and antibiotics that need a prescription in the USA or northern Europe are available over the counter in Nicaragua, if you know what you need.

For anything serious, especially where scans and laboratory tests are needed, head for a modern hospital in Managua such as the highly recommended Hospital Metropolitano Vivian Pellas, which offers emergency facilities and all the medical treatments you would expect at a high-quality hospital in the US or Europe. Prices in private hospitals are lower than in the US, and increasing numbers of US nationals are coming to the country for cosmetic surgery, hip replacements, and other surgical procedures that cost more at home.

Expatriates who intend to stay living or working in Nicaragua for a long time should take out private health insurance, either through their employer or on their own. The Vivian Pellas Hospital also offers its own corporate and individual health plans that include regular check-ups for a fixed fee.

BE INSURED

Before you travel, make sure you have adequate insurance to cover treatment in case of accident or illness. It pays to read the small print to find out what is and isn't covered. Take out a policy that covers emergency medical transport, evacuation, and repatriation, especially if you plan to travel to remote places along the Rio San Juan or the Atlantic coast where medical services are limited, or to take part in strenuous outdoor activities.

Health Precautions

Nicaragua is a hot, tropical country with year-round sunshine due to its position above the Equator. At the height of the dry season in April and May temperatures can reach a sweltering 100°F (38°C). Sunburn is not an issue only on the Pacific lowlands or Atlantic beaches, but also in the higher coffee-growing regions of Matagalpa. Take basic precautions and wear sun cream with a high protection factor, reapplying it regularly. Plan activities for early or late in the day, when the sun is less fierce. Drink plenty of liquids and wear a hat to avoid sunstroke, especially on boat trips where the sun is reflected off the water or when climbing volcanoes, where there is little shade.

Avoid tap water. Stick to bottled water, which is cheap and available in most places. If you are traveling to remote spots, take sufficient bottled water with you.

Traveler's diarrhea is a possibility, so pack Lomotil or a similar product, which will help if you need to take a long journey on a chicken bus, or a flight. Drink plenty of water and use rehydration salts to aid recovery. Usually, diarrhea clears up on its own and is just a reaction to a change in diet and hot weather. Street food is best eaten piping hot straight off the grill. Avoid green salads and don't overindulge in exotic fruits and fruit juices. The secret is to eat lightly, and keep up your fluid intake.

Vaccinations

As a general precaution, some vaccination clinics recommend a tetanus-diphtheria booster if you haven't had one in the last ten years. The Centers for Disease Control and Prevention also recommend you to have vaccinations against typhoid and Hepatitis A. If you

TOILET ETIQUETTE

There's a whole ritual to what happens in the smallest room in the house (or in the yard in many instances in Nicaragua). While it might seem like business as usual in Nicaragua's top hotels, what you will quickly come to realize is that there is a range of experiences awaiting you behind the doors of the country's *baños* (restrooms), especially if you intend to do a home-stay or volunteer in a rural area. First of all, due to small plumbing pipes that block easily, toilet paper is not flushed but deposited in a trashcan by the side of the *inodoro* (toilet). Also, be warned that not all *inodoros* will have seats (so those yoga classes will come in handy). The norm in rural areas is to have an outdoor toilet, or *letrina* (latrine), which is probably best tackled in a speedy fashion, and with a fully charged torch at night. Where water is scarce a bucket by the side is usually provided for flushing. It might seem a chore, but it is considered bad form not to flush, and if you take time to refill the bucket you'll score bonus points with your hosts. Carry a small roll of *papel higiénico* (toilet paper) for emergencies.

think you might have "sex with a new partner, get a tattoo or piercing, or have any medical procedures," you should also consider getting a jab for Hepatitis B. There is no requirement to have a yellow fever vaccination unless you are arriving in Nicaragua from a country with a recent outbreak.

Insect-Borne Diseases

Most travelers to Nicaragua are unaffected by mosquito-borne viruses, but there is a risk of contracting dengue, chikungunya, or zika, which are all tropical fevers spread by biting mosquitoes known generically in Nicaragua as *zancudos*. There are no vaccinations against these virus infections, so prevention of bites is the key. Mosquitoes are most active around sunset, so apply a liquid repellent like DEET, and wear long sleeves and long pants. If you can, sleep with the air conditioning on, or under a mosquito net, especially in mosquito hotspots like the RACCN and RACCS autonomous regions.

Dengue is known as break-bone fever, due to the pain felt in joints in extreme cases, but it usually clears up without complications. Dengue hemorrhagic fever is a more aggressive form that can require medical attention, especially in children, but is less prevalent.

Nicaragua has also seen sporadic outbreaks of chikungunya and zika in some parts of the country. The zika virus has been linked to serious birth defects like microcephaly, and pregnant women are warned not to travel to areas affected with the virus. It can also be passed through sexual contact with an infected person, so to avoid infection practice safe sex and use condoms.

There is a very low risk of malaria in Chinandega, Jinotega, León, Managua, Matagalpa, the RACCN, and the RACCS. Volunteers facing a long posting in malarial areas should consider taking preventive medication such as chloroquine or mefloquine.

Natural Dangers

Nicaragua is a land that has seen more than its fair share of natural disasters—a consequence of its position on the Pacific Ring of Fire and the heavy rains that buffet the country during the Caribbean hurricane season. It has at least six active volcanoes. The chances of being caught up in a deadly eruption are slim, given today's sophisticated monitoring equipment and Nicaragua's well-rehearsed evacuation measures, but hikers and climbers should always seek up-to-date advice before setting out on a trek to the summit of an active volcano.

EMERGENCY NUMBERS

Local Emergency: 118 or *911 from a cell phone (Spanish only)
National Police: 118
Fire Department: 115
Red Cross (ambulance): 128
Be aware that ambulance response times can be slow, especially outside Managua, and in some cases nonexistent. If you need to get to a hospital fast, a taxi may be the best option. Heed local advice on what to do in an emergency.

SAFETY

Nicaragua is the safest country in Central America, and the second-safest country in Latin America after Uruguay, but caution should always be exercised by visitors, especially in the first few days of their visit. Never carry anything you cannot afford to lose or cannot claim back on your travel insurance. The main threats to tourists are petty opportunist crimes like pick-pocketing and the snatching of bags, phones, or cameras. Sensible precautions should always be taken.

Take particular care of your belongings when traveling by bus or taxi, when arriving at new destinations, and in crowded places such as markets and bus stations in Managua, Granada, Masaya, and Estelí.

At night it is not advisable to walk in Managua alone, although great efforts have been made to increase illumination and security in the area around the Old Cathedral and the Plaza de la Revolución. Instead, take taxis to and from restaurants and nightspots. The fairly new Puerto Salvador Allende is a lakeside complex of restaurants and bars where you can enjoy the evening breeze in a secure environment.

Outside Managua, crime tends to be opportunistic, so keep an eye on your valuables at all times. There have been reports of muggings at night on beaches along the Pacific coast and in the small towns on the Atlantic coast. Even on the tiny Caribbean island of Little Corn there have been reports of tourists having valuables stolen while walking along lonely paths. But these incidents are isolated. Always heed advice from locals.

Caution should be taken when traveling through the towns of Siuna, Bonanza, and La Rosita in the so-called Mining Triangle where there have been reports of theft.

Backpackers and budget travelers should consider carrying a "mugger's wallet" with some low-denomination bills and coins for small purchases, and hiding their main pouch or money belt under their clothes. Money should be stashed in different pockets, and daypacks should be on the chest.

Business travelers and tourists should always check the latest safety warnings from the Web site of their embassy, or visit the Web sites of the US State Department (http://travel.state.gov/content/passports/english/country/nicaragua.html) or UK Foreign Office (https://www.gov.uk/foreign-travel-advice/nicaragua).

TIPS ON STAYING SAFE

- Don't attract the attention of thieves. Leave jewelry at home and keep cameras and phones out of sight.
- Don't use ATMs in the street or at night. Try to use ATMs inside banks during the day.
- Travel with others. You are safer in a group, and solo travelers, especially women, may be targeted.
- Learn some Spanish.
- Listen to the locals. Heed advice on places to avoid, and don't go to the poor areas of major cities.
- Know where you are going. Don't wander around with a map looking lost.
- Take taxis at night, and always use official taxis with red-bordered number plates.
- Avoid crowds. Don't travel on city buses in Managua during peak hours with anything you don't want to lose. Pickpockets, including minors, will take advantage of the crush. Also in markets.
- Use the hotel safe. Don't walk around with all your cash, but have something to hand over if mugged.
- Let it go. If you are held up by an armed assailant, hand over your stuff. Keep calm and don't resist.
- Have a backup. Keep emergency bills hidden in your belt, shoes, etc., just in case.
- Carry a "mugger's wallet." This is a decoy wallet with a few small bills and coins for minor purchases, and an expired credit card and/or an old library or gym card for authenticity.
- Copy documents. Scan your passport, airline tickets, and insurance documents, and e-mail yourself and family or friends a copy. Include the details of your bank and credit card companies so that you can quickly cancel the cards in case of theft or loss.

chapter eight

BUSINESS BRIEFING

THE BUSINESS LANDSCAPE

After decades in the doldrums following the Sandinista Revolution, the drawn-out and devastating Contra War, and a series of natural disasters that set back progress, Nicaragua has turned the economy around in recent years and is open for business.

Since the Sandinistas returned to power in 2007, the country has seen ten years of stability and an opening to private enterprise that has helped the economy grow by roughly 5 percent a year between 2012 and 2018, outstripping most other countries in Latin America.

Low wages, tax incentives, an increase in local purchasing power, and the benefits of Nicaragua's membership in the Central American–Dominican Republic Free Trade Agreement (CAFTA–DR), have all encouraged foreign firms from North America, Europe, and Asia to set up shop in the country.

The government has created more than forty Free Trade Zones—industrial parks located near ports and major cities where factories turn out textiles, clothes, and cigars, and pack bananas, all for export. The Free Trade Zone regime has become the most dynamic sector of the national economy and has been expanded to encompass call centers and technology companies.

The sectors that have most benefited from foreign investment include tourism, telecommunications, the service industry, mining, agri-business, and renewable energy initiatives such as wind turbines and geothermal power generated from the country's active volcanoes.

Nicaragua's homegrown staples have also seen a boom. The excellent quality of the country's coffee, cocoa beans, tobacco, bananas, beef, and shrimp are now recognized around the world, and have attracted growing interest from foreign entrepreneurs in the USA, Europe, Asia, and elsewhere in Latin America.

Despite a sometimes rocky political relationship with the US government over the last few years, Nicaragua has actively encouraged US companies to operate in the country. The country's most widely dispersed supermarket chain, Palí, and the hypermarket Maxi-Palí stores, are operated by US firm Walmart, which also runs the upscale supermarket chain La Unión and has now opened two large outlets in Managua under its own name. Franchised US food chains, including McDonald's, Pizza Hut, Papa John's, Subway, and Hooters, can be found in shiny modern malls in Managua, and are artfully tucked away in historic

buildings in colonial cities like Granada and León so as not to spoil the aesthetic.

Another important element in Nicaragua's business landscape is the expat community—the large numbers of US, Canadian, and European nationals who have relocated to tourism hotspots like Granada, San Juan del Sur, León, Esteli, Matagalpa, and the Corn Islands.

Hotels, resorts, surf schools, yoga camps, restaurants, bars, micro-breweries, and real estate ventures run by expats have played a significant part in Nicaragua's tourism boom and have brought in new business models and a greater diversification of tourism-related products and services to the country.

DOING BUSINESS IN NICARAGUA

The rewards of doing business in Nicaragua can be great. It's an emerging market with a growing internal economy that offers a wide range of opportunities and start-up incentives for switched-on entrepreneurs who are prepared to do their homework. Since the 1990s a whole-scale privatization of state-run enterprises has created a much more dynamic private sector. Family-run businesses are still very much the norm, usually focused on one area or product. The exception is Grupo Pellas, run by Nicaragua's first billionaire, Carlos Pellas, a huge conglomerate of more than twenty companies involved in everything from Flor de Caña rum and sugar production to banking, insurance, automotive sales, media, health care, and tourism.

The first step for anybody interested in learning about local business opportunities is to contact the business attaché in their country's consulate or embassy in Nicaragua. They will usually have an up-to-date list of local firms who can offer legal advice and translate contracts. Local chambers of commerce can be useful.

The paperwork involved in setting up a business will take a little longer than in North America or Europe, but the government has created a one-stop-shop to facilitate the process run by the Ministerio de Fomento, Industria y Comercio (MIFIC). Nicaragua also has its own business promotion office called ProNicaragua, which can help potential investors.

Personal Relationships
Who you know and how you come across is nearly as important as the strength of your business proposal in Latin America, and Nicaragua is no exception. In the past, a small elite of rich families controlled the country, so if you wanted to meet the decision makers and get deals done all you needed was an impressive last name or the right friends. While times have changed, the etiquette of doing business still revolves around building personal relationships, which is not really possible to do by email, or with the kind of fly-in-fly-out approach that might work in Germany or Canada.

The key is to get to know the right people, and keeping contacts fresh once you have established a connection. Networking and face-to-face contact (in person rather than on Facebook) will be crucial to the success of any venture you embark upon in Nicaragua.

Initial meetings will often ignore the business at hand and revolve around friendly chitchat about your family, your home town, and what you think of Nicaragua. Very often you will need several visits before you see any results. This might be frustrating for foreign executives used to a faster turnaround, but trying to rush negotiations could be perceived negatively, so it's important to slow down, and factor in enough time.

Dress Code

Nicaraguans are very accepting, but first impressions count, and it pays to dress well at initial encounters. At top-level meetings and business-related social events with multinationals and large conglomerates in Managua formal business wear of dark suit and tie for men and a similarly formal outfit for women are the norm, but elsewhere the rules are more relaxed. The sub-tropical heat dictates the dress code to some extent. For men, a tropical-style *guayabera* shirt or even short sleeves are perfectly acceptable, as long as the overall impression is neat, and for women, dresses, skirts, and pants are all appropriate attire.

Treat breakfast and lunch meetings as formal, unless told otherwise, and dress appropriately for evening events or dinner, depending on the venue.

WOMEN IN BUSINESS

Nicaragua scores highly on international surveys of gender equality, and has done much to increase the percentage of women at all levels in government and government-run entities. In the private sector, while many of the top CEOs are men, female professionals now make up a significant percentage of middle-management roles. An increasing number of women are achieving higher degrees at university, and female entrepreneurs are making their mark in a wide range of industries, including public relations, marketing, fashion, and design.

Many medium-sized and small businesses are run by women, especially retail stores and food outlets. In the informal sector, food and market stalls are predominantly run by women.

Foreign women coming to do business in Nicaragua are unlikely to encounter any problems, although they may find some local attitudes to women old-fashioned and even quaint. The key is always to keep things professional, friendly, and polite.

When meeting a Nicaraguan woman in a business environment for the first time, a warm handshake is the best approach. At subsequent meetings, and as the relationship develops, a quick kiss on the cheek is typical among Nicaraguans, but don't attempt it as a foreigner if you don't feel comfortable.

SETTING UP A MEETING

One of the challenges in Nicaragua is finding out who has the power to sign off on the deals you want to do. The next challenge is to find a way to get hold of that person and arrange a face-to-face meeting.

Setting up a meeting with a government body can be a drawn-out process if you haven't been to Nicaragua before and don't have local contacts. Start at your local Nicaraguan embassy, with a formal letter or email in Spanish outlining your interests and explaining your background. ProNicaragua, the government's business promotion office, should also be able to help. Also, if you can get the trade attaché at your own country's embassy in Nicaragua or local partners or agents to help you with contacts, things should move faster.

If you are approaching a large Nicaraguan firm used to dealing with foreign companies, send a direct e-mail or letter in Spanish proposing possible dates for a personal meeting. This should be followed up by an e-mail and phone call about two weeks prior to the meeting to make sure everything is on schedule, and another courtesy call the day before the meeting just to check in and confirm. This might seem like overkill, but in Nicaragua things can change quite quickly and businesspeople might be juggling many things at the same time. It's important to keep contacts fresh, remind people you're coming, and build a rapport.

If you want a quick outcome it's best to come to Nicaragua and meet people in person. Entrepreneurs who have spent months sending out e-mails from their home country without any concrete response will find that, once in Nicaragua, they will start to see results. Nicaraguans prefer to deal with people face-to-face, and once they know you personally will be more likely to introduce you to other business acquaintances and help you to set up meetings.

Timing
Many business meetings in Nicaragua are scheduled for the morning. Depending on the size of the company, you may be invited to a breakfast meeting with several executives and decision makers where you can discuss things over coffee and a pastry. These often

act simply as pre-meetings, and are a chance to find out more about you, so don't be frustrated if you don't get down to business straight away. This is not the time to get a decision. The same holds true for lunch meetings. A detailed breakdown of your proposal might have to wait until a pitch meeting.

An invitation to dinner, especially on your first night in town, is more likely to be a hospitable gesture than a desire to do business with you there and then. Remain professional at all times, even when out on the town.

It's usual for the person who issues the invitation to pay the bill. You may offer to pick up the tab, but never offer to pay just your share, which would come over as rude and tight-fisted. Neither should you insist too hard on paying, as this may cause offense. It's better to let your host pay, and show your appreciation by returning the invitation for the next meal.

An important consideration when scheduling appointments is that Nicaraguans take their weekends and public holidays seriously, and there is little chance of getting anything done on a Monday morning, a Friday afternoon, or during the long holiday periods around Christmas, the New Year, or Easter. The days before, during, and after Liberation Day in July and Independence Day in September should also be avoided, if possible, as it is hard to get anything done during these national celebrations.

Punctuality

Latin America is often portrayed in books, films, and the media as a land of *mañana* ("tomorrow"), where the usual rules of punctuality don't apply. Nicaragua has its own version of this stereotype, known as "Nica time," a perception that Nicaraguans have a more flexible and forgiving attitude to time and that people being late for things is to be expected. This laid-back approach to punctuality may hark back to Nicaragua's rural past, when farm work moved to a slower, more natural rhythm, with bursts of frantic activity during harvest time followed by relative inactivity. Nicaraguans rely on family, neighbors, and coworkers to help them get by when times are tough. Setting aside time to attend to family issues and social obligations is a natural part of living in highly interconnected communities, and should be understood in that context.

Other commentators have put the vagaries of "Nica time" down to the intense, energy-sapping heat that many Nicaraguans live with, the traffic jams that snarl up Managua and other cities at peak times, or simply the fact that Nicaraguans spend more time on social niceties as they go about their daily business.

In practical terms, a certain amount of leeway should always be factored in when arranging business meetings, to allow for last-minute scheduling hiccups. If you do have to wait, even for an hour or so, or even reschedule a meeting for another day, this is nothing personal. It's just a local peculiarity that you will have to get used to. The important thing is not to show undue annoyance when last-minute changes occur, and to make sure you leave room in your schedule for contingencies.

Foreigners wanting to do business in Nicaragua, however, should always make sure that they arrive at the appointed hour for a meeting, and should factor in potential transport delays when making their plans.

MEETINGS AND PRESENTATIONS

Meetings usually begin with a formal introduction to each person in the room, and it is polite to offer a general greeting to the group of "*Buenos dias*" or "*Buenas tardes*," according to the time of day. Nicaraguans shake hands when meeting, and use the expression "*Mucho gusto*" ("Pleased to meet you") or "*Es un placer conocerle*" ("It's a pleasure to meet you"). It is customary to exchange business cards.

Any material or brochures you bring with you should be translated into Spanish, preferably by a translator who has experience of Nicaraguan expressions. This is to avoid the use of any words used in another Spanish-speaking country that don't convey the right meaning or tone in Nicaragua.

Senior executives in large private companies may speak good English, but there's no guarantee of this, so you will need an interpreter or intermediary who can translate for you, even if some people in the room do speak English. When dealing with government agencies you should always bring an interpreter, and preferably a clear outline of your proposal written in Spanish. Presentations should also be given in Spanish, preferably with an interpreter who can convey all the subtleties of your pitch if your Spanish is not up to it.

Questions may be asked in a very direct way, but don't take this as confrontational. Give calm, measured responses. The key is to remain friendly and professional at all times. Don't be put off if there is conversation during your presentation, or if people take phone calls or leave the room while you are speaking. This is just another example of a more relaxed attitude to doing business.

NEGOTIATIONS

Having given your pitch and answered questions, don't expect an immediate answer, as several meetings will usually be needed before a final deal is reached. You will often be told that somebody else has to be consulted, and when dealing with government agencies that is probably the case, but in private firms this could also be a polite way of saying, "We'll think about it."

If negotiations drag on too long, however, it probably means that the Nicaraguan side is avoiding a straight "No" in favor of subtle hints. Having local contacts who are more used to the subtleties of Nicaraguan negotiations will help you to interpret their responses.

CONTRACTS AND LEGAL CONSIDERATIONS

Certain commercial rights such as repatriation of profits, non-discriminatory treatment relative to local investors, and protection from expropriation are enshrined under the CAFTA–DR free trade agreement between Central America, the Dominican Republic, and the USA. Nicaragua also has a Foreign Investment Law, which offers a protective framework for foreign firms wishing to do business in the country.

Nevertheless, it is advisable to seek guidance from a well-respected law firm on all the legal issues pertaining to any potential business venture before you start. Local lawyers can offer invaluable advice on local labor laws and are essential when drawing up draft contracts in Spanish and English. They can also help iron out any contractual issues before you sign on the dotted line. In particular, when investing in real estate or land, a local lawyer should be engaged to check that land titles and registrations are legally held and there are no discrepancies with property borders or rights of access.

Your country's embassy or business chamber in Nicaragua will have up-to-date information on the legal status of foreign firms in Nicaragua, and should be able to provide information about reliable local law firms.

MANAGING DISAGREEMENTS

If disagreements arise over a contract or payment, the first and best option is to try to deal with it straight away. Good legal advice is essential before embarking on any venture, as going to court over a contract breach can be a slow and protracted process. The best way to avoid disputes is to maintain frequent contact with Nicaraguan business partners, which will help to build strong personal ties and flag up issues before disputes arise. This may mean a closer working relationship than you would foster with a business partner in the USA or UK, and more time spent on the ground.

MANAGEMENT STYLE

While many Nicaraguan managers have taken business degrees in the USA, and many firms operating in Nicaragua employ US management styles, the traditional hierarchy of a family business is still very much the norm. The boss in Nicaragua is definitely the boss, and below him or her there will be several management levels, layered one upon another.

Formality and the use of titles is fairly widespread, and politeness is important. When addressing clients use the polite *Señor* or *Señora* with their last name, for example, Señor Lopez, rather than assuming you are on first-name terms. When speaking to them in Spanish, remember to use *usted* (the formal singular form of "you") rather than the less formal *tu* (the informal singular form) or the chummy *vos* (the informal singular of "you" used among friends by most Nicaraguans).

You will also hear local workers refer to their boss using deferential terms such as *mi estimado/a* (esteemed one) or as *Don* or *Doña* (which is used with first names, such as Don Pedro or Doña Maria). However, to avoid offense a foreigner should use these terms cautiously until a personal relationship is established.

It might sound strange to non-Latin Americans but it is also typical for an engineer to be addressed as *Ingeniero*, a university graduate as *Licenciado*, and a businessman with a Master's degree to be addressed as *Doctor*. Very often the title will be included on their business card. Foreign businesspeople will not be expected to use these terms, but they do give an insight into the pecking order in a company, and knowing them will certainly help if you are thinking of setting up a business and employing Nicaraguans.

A foreign businessperson managing Nicaraguan staff will be expected to act as a boss and maintain a certain distance with staff, while exhibiting enough empathy for them to be able to express their concerns.

Nicaragua has strict labor laws, and foreign managers will need to be up to speed with the specific regulations on the minimum wage, end of year bonus provisions, maternity leave entitlements, and how to handle disciplinary procedures.

DEALING WITH RED TAPE

While great strides have been taken in Nicaragua to streamline and hasten the process of setting up a business, there will still be times when dealing with government entities can be frustrating. One way to speed things up is to work with local partners, business associations, or reputable agencies who already have contacts and can cut down the time it takes to negotiate the necessary red tape. For importing or exporting goods through customs, a reputable local agent is essential.

CORRUPTION

Nicaragua has been cracking down on corruption, and foreigners doing business in Nicaragua should always steer clear of any individual or company that offers a short cut to official procedures through any form of inducement, whether financial or in kind.

GIFT GIVING

There is no obligation to give gifts, but something typical from your country—attractively wrapped confectionery, a bottle of wine or whiskey, or a coffee-table book featuring glossy photos of your city or country—can act as a good icebreaker when first meeting potential clients in Nicaragua.

Equally, a potential client might present you with a bottle of the country's premium Flor de Caña rum, a typical craft item, or a selection of top-quality Nicaraguan coffee, chocolates, or cigars.

Gifts and treating clients to hospitality are not illegal in Nicaragua, and many Nicaraguan businesses will send out small gifts to clients and customers at Christmas, or to celebrate an anniversary. However, it is best not to give expensive gifts that could be misinterpreted as bribes. Some large multinationals operating in the country do not allow staff to accept gifts, for the same reason.

chapter nine

COMMUNICATING

LANGUAGE

The official language of Nicaragua is Spanish, which is the first language of more than 90 percent of the population. Nicaraguan Spanish is known as *Nicañol*, which has its own lively rhythm and rich vocabulary.

Along the Atlantic coast, in Bluefields, Pearl Lagoon, and the Corn Islands, Creole English predominates. This is a legacy of the British presence along the Mosquito Coast in the eighteenth and nineteenth centuries, and a long history of trading links with the English-speaking islands of the Caribbean.

Miskito (or Miskitu) is spoken by the indigenous communities along the Rio Coco, on the border with Honduras, and along the Mosquito Coast. Part of the Native American Misumalpan language family, Miskito also uses words from English, Creole, and Spanish.

Nicaragua has a small but culturally significant mixed-race Garifuna population in coastal towns in the Pearl Lagoon. In 2008 the UN declared the Garifuna language—a combination of Arawak and Carib—a Masterpiece of the Oral and Intangible Heritage of Humanity. After a period of decline, Garifuna communities in Belize, Guatemala, Honduras, and Nicaragua are now working together to keep their culture and language alive.

Even in areas where indigenous groups maintain their own languages as a first language, almost everybody will speak and understand Spanish, which is the language of government and the principal language taught in schools.

In recognition of the cultural history of the Atlantic coast, Creole, Miskito, Sumu, Rama, and Garifuna are accepted as official languages within the RACCN and RACCS autonomous regions.

Speaking Spanish

If you want to meet the locals and learn about their lives you will need to learn at least a little Spanish. From primary school onward, all Nicaraguan children learn English as part of the national curriculum, and most will be able to form simple questions such as: "How are you?" "What is your name?" and "Where are you from?" In general, however, unless you are on the Atlantic coast or the Corn Islands, where Creole English is the lingua franca, the only people who will be able to converse with you in English are hotel staff, tourist guides, and Nicaraguans who have spent time working or studying in the USA.

Being able to deliver a few key phrases, typical menu items, and some local slang will not only boost your confidence but will also be greatly appreciated. Start with a simple greeting like *Hola!* (Hello!), and learn a local expression like *Ideay?* ("What's happening?")

When you sit down to a meal, say to the other diners "*Buen provecho*" (Enjoy your meal), and let the cook know that your food was "*Sabroso, gracias!*" (Delicious, thank you!). If you are asked what you think of Nicaragua, you'll get a smile if you say it's *tuani* or *diacachimba*, which both mean "Cool!"

If you plan to spend some time in the country, there are good schools teaching Spanish to foreigners in Granada, San Juan del Sur, Estelí, and Managua. Some schools offer home-stays with a Nicaraguan family, which is a great way to fast-track your Spanish and get a real insight into the food, culture, and daily life of the locals.

Speaking Like a Local

The Spanish spoken in Nicaragua is sometimes referred to as *Nicañol,* or Nica, but, apart from an abundance of local vocabulary that makes it unique, it follows the rules and conventions of classic *Castellano,* the Castilian Spanish brought to the New World in the sixteenth century by the conquistadors.

The first difference you'll notice between *Nicañol* and the Spanish spoken in modern-day Madrid is that there is no lisp on the letters *c* or *z*. So, *cerveza* (beer) is pronounced sir-vay-sir, and *gracias* (thank you) is pronounced gra-si-ass.

Nicaraguan Spanish is also characterized by *voseo*—the use of *vos* as the informal second person singular pronoun instead of *tú*, which is known as *tuteo*. *Voseo* is widespread across Central America, as it is in Argentina and Uruguay, and in Nicaragua is used on TV, in adverts, and on advertising billboards. A campaign to encourage absent fathers to participate in their children's upbringing used the slogan: "*Vos sos mi papá*" (You are my dad). Anybody who has learned Spanish using *tú* will be understood in Nicaragua, but may find it confusing at first to hear all the *vos* endings on verbs.

As in other Spanish-speaking countries, the formal second person singular pronoun *usted* is used when speaking to elders or superiors to show respect.

SAY HELLO, SAY GOOD-BYE

Nicaragua is one of the few countries in Latin America where you'll be greeted with "Good-bye"! *Adiós* is normally used as a farewell in most Spanish-speaking countries, but in rural areas of Nicaragua it's a common way to say hello when you're passing by and don't have time to chat.

Everyday Courtesies

Having good manners and showing respect for others is very important in Nicaragua. When entering a shop or office, people will say to those present "*Buenos días*" (Good morning), "*Buenas tardes*" (Good afternoon), or "*Buenas noches*" (Good evening). A simple "*Buenas*" will do in most situations, whatever the time of day.

You can also show respect by addressing or referring to people as *Señor/Señora*, and to the elderly by using *Don/Doña* with their first name. *Señorita* is the equivalent of Miss in English (there is no equivalent of Ms.). If you don't know a woman's marital status the best policy is to use *Señorita* with younger women, and let them correct you.

When being introduced it is customary to say "*Mucho gusto*" (Pleased to meet you), or "*Un placer*" (A pleasure), and your first name, to introduce yourself.

SPEAKING ENGLISH

As we have seen, primary schools have started teaching English in order to equip students with a foreign language that would be useful for business and tourism. The tourism sector has seen rapid growth in the last ten years, with visitor numbers rising from around a million

SPEAK LIKE A NICA

Textbook Spanish will help you get by in Nicaragua, but to fit in with new friends a few typical words and phrases can go a long way. Use slang expressions with caution, and gauge your audience beforehand. Not all Nicaraguans use the same expressions, and a word that provokes mirth among a group of friends might cause offense in polite company.

Cachimbazo de agua or *Vergazo de agua*: Heavy rain
Chavalo/chavala: Boy/girl
Cipote: Kid
Chocho!: Wow!
Chele/Chela: Light-skinned person or foreigner
Chunche: Thingummyjig (can be used for anything)
Dale pues: Go for it. Let's do it. A confirmation.
Diacachimba: Cool!
Fachento: Stuck up, arrogant
Goma: Hangover
Ipegüe (Ee-peg-way): An added extra. At the market you might ask a stallholder to throw in an extra banana or mango, with the expression: *Y el ipegüe?*
Maje (Ma-hey): Dude
Oe (Oh-eh): Hey
Palmado: Broke, skint
Pinche: Mean, stingy
Pinolero/Pinolera: Nicaraguan
Puchica!: Wow (in a negative sense)! Damn!
Prix: Buddy, mate
Que nota, prix? : What's up, buddy?
Salvaje!: Excellent, cool! (literally, savage)
Tapudo: A big mouth, liar
Tuani : Cool!

to well over 1.5 million in 2018. In business, Nicaragua has seen many call centers open, taking advantage of tax breaks and low start-up costs, which has also fueled a demand for more English-speakers.

On the Atlantic coast and on the Corn Islands, where English Creole is commonly spoken, communication with the locals is no problem for English-speaking visitors. Likewise in tourist resorts such as San Juan del Sur, and the cities of Granada and León, it is not too hard to find somebody with some command of English. But this is less likely in rural areas.

One advantage of the growing interest in English for the visitor is that many locals will want to practice their English-language skills on you, and may reciprocate by teaching you a few words or phrases in Spanish. It also means that there are plenty of opportunities to help out at schools and colleges for those want to volunteer.

BODY LANGUAGE

In general, Nicaraguans are slightly more reserved than Cubans or Argentinians when interacting, particularly in the rural north and in indigenous communities, but they do use body language to communicate, and it is important to understand the gestures they use.

Pointing with the lips is a gesture that can confuse newcomers but is typical all over Nicaragua. Ask somebody where something is, and they will pucker up and point it out with their pursed lips.

Nicaraguans also scrunch up the nose to indicate that they don't understand what you are saying.

To indicate that someone is being tight-fisted or mean with money, it is typical to bend the arm up and tap the elbow, which comes from the expression *No seas codo* (literally, "don't be elbow"), although you are

SPEAK LIKE A MISKITO

Apart from Spanish and English Creole, the main indigenous language in Nicaragua is Miskito, with some 150,000 speakers. The influence of English and Creole along the Mosquito Coast can be heard today in the Miskito words for illness (*siknes*), please (*plees*) and the generic Caribbean morning greeting *mar'ning*. If you visit one of the stilt-house Miskito communities near Bilwi, or a village on the banks of the Rio Coco, here are a few words and phrases to try out.

Nak'sa: Hello
Yan nini ... : My name is ...
Yamni balram: Welcome
Aisabe: Goodbye
Kai ki was: See you later
Ti tan yamni: Good morning
Tut ni yamni: Good afternoon
Thimia yamni: Good evening
Pain (p-eye-n): Good
Saura: Bad
Naki preis?: How much?
Tinki pali: Thank you

more likely to hear the expression *No seas pinche*, which means the same.

Extending your index fingers and rubbing one over the other, as if you were peeling a carrot, indicates that it's time to pay, and it can be used in a restaurant to ask for the bill, or might be used by workers to remind the boss that it's pay day.

Holding out the hands to show your flat palms is a way of saying *Estoy palmado* (I'm broke), and is a good gesture to use when being hassled to buy something in the street or in a market.

It can be considered rude or aggressive to point directly at somebody with your finger or to beckon somebody over to you with your fingers pointing upwards, like a cop directing traffic. Nicaraguans do it with the palm facing downward and the fingers pointing down, like a one-handed doggy paddle.

Personal Space
Nicaraguans feel comfortable being physically closer to each other than many people in the US or northern Europe would. Once introduced, they kiss on the cheek, shake hands, and even backslap on subsequent meetings, depending on their feelings at meeting again. The etiquette between women, or between a man and a woman, is a single kiss on the right cheek. This is not a romantic kiss, just a touch of the cheeks, or an air kiss.

THE MEDIA
Newspapers, radio, and terrestrial, cable, and satellite TV all contribute to a fairly diverse Nicaraguan media scene that is gradually moving online. The growth of Wi-Fi access and the arrival of 3G and 4G signals mean that many Nicaraguans can now use cell phones and tablets to access newspaper Web sites, social media, and streaming video services. However, low incomes and large families still prevent the poorest in Nicaragua from accessing new technologies.

Television
The first TV stations in Nicaragua began broadcasting in the mid 1950s, and were closely linked to the Somoza regime. Following the Sandinista Revolution the new

government created dedicated state-run TV channels to inform and educate the population and promote Nicaraguan art, music, and culture. This formatting style continues today on the government-run Channel 4, and Channels 6, 8, and 13, although 8 is targeted at a young audience and shows a variety of US series.

In the main cities and towns, access to satellite or cable TV from companies such as Claro and Sky offers a greater choice of programming and a large selection of English-language movies, news, sports, and entertainment channels from the USA and the UK. The arrival of streaming video services like Netflix, offering instant access to the latest TV series and movies, has shaken up the local market as more Nicaraguans get their TV fix online.

Radio

Hundreds of radio stations across Nicaragua cater to every musical interest, and broadcast a wide range of local news, sports, religious messages, and advertising. Some remote rural communities still live without electricity, relying on battery or solar-powered radios for their news and entertainment. Radio also remains an important means of communication for the country's countless religious groups, and many Churches, big and small, operate radio stations to spread the word.

On the Atlantic coast and Nicaragua's Caribbean Corn Islands, stations broadcasting in Miskito and Creole play an important role in keeping these languages alive.

Newspapers

There are only a few newspapers in circulation in Nicaragua. *La Prensa* is a conservative newspaper owned by the Chamorro family, and *El Nuevo Diario* is considered left-leaning. *Hoy* features celebrity gossip and lurid crime stories, and *Metro* is a free paper in Managua. Old Sandinista publications such as *Barricada* have closed down to be replaced by online media like *El 19* and the Web site of *La Voz del Sandinismo*.

SERVICES
Telephone
Landlines in Nicaragua offer cheap rates for local calls, but it can be a lengthy and costly process to have one installed, and is impossible in some rural areas, so Nicaraguans increasingly rely on cell phones. The most popular contract or pay-as-you-go services are Movistar and Claro. Competition for users has seen prices fall, but as calls made from a Movistar account to a Claro account cost more than a Movistar to Movistar call, many people carry two phones or a double SIM card, to switch depending on the number they are calling. Where there is free Wi-Fi, Nicaraguans avoid charges by using social media Apps like WhatsApp.

North Americans or Europeans who want to avoid roaming charges can buy a local Sim card and top it up with $10 or $20 for use in Nicaragua, but the phone must be unlocked.

Internet
Nicaragua is only just starting to plug its six million people into the Internet at home on broadband services. In the meantime, smart phones are the main means of access to the Internet via cell phone data packages or free Wi-Fi provided by local authorities in public squares. A campaign to provide a Wi-Fi enabled park in

every town and village of Nicaragua has also helped to bring free Wi-Fi to remote rural areas, although the farther into the wild you go, the less chance you have of connecting.

There is no charge to use the Wi-Fi in hotels, restaurants, or cafés. Wi-Fi signals are generally strong enough to upload photos and post on social media.

Free Wi-Fi and smart phone access has led to the gradual demise of the once ubiquitous Internet café. However, if you'd rather tap out e-mails on an antiquated PC with some of the letters rubbed off the keyboard, or need to print something out, you can still find the odd Internet café, usually crowded with kids doing schoolwork or playing online games. Some Internet cafés also have phone booths where you can make international calls more cheaply than from your hotel.

Social media Apps like WhatsApp, Twitter, Snapchat, and Instagram are popular in Nicaragua, but Facebook leads the field, with almost as many registered users as Internet users. It might sound counterintuitive, but some hotels and resorts respond more quickly to messages sent via their Facebook pages than they do to traditional e-mails.

Mail

Smart phones and the Internet have had a massive impact on the quantity of mail sent around the world, but sometimes paper documents or products you've bought online need to be delivered. In Nicaragua, the public postal service, Correos de Nicaragua, offers cheap rates for stamps, but mail to North America or Europe can take a month. Local postal deliveries have a less than perfect reputation, and sometimes fail to arrive at all, perhaps because of the lack of mailboxes at people's homes, or perhaps because postal workers are just confused by the country's arcane address system and the lack of street names and numbers.

To minimize delivery problems, Nicaraguans can rent a post office box at their local post office and pick up items from there, although many people simply hand-deliver items themselves, or put them on a bus to be picked up by the recipient at the other end.

To receive parcels sent from abroad, Nicaraguans use private courier companies such as DHL, TransExpress Nicaragua, or AeroCasillas. Bear in mind that any valuable goods, including electronic devices, and medicines, are taxed heavily on entry, and it may be cheaper to purchase an alternative locally.

CONCLUSION

Nicaragua is identified in the popular imagination by the Sandinista Revolution: the striking news images of Molotov cocktails wielded by fresh-faced students, the barricades blocking the streets, the ordinary people coming together to topple a brutal dictatorship, the meddling hand of the USA, the thousands of well-meaning *brigadistas* who came to help sustain the literary campaign during the Contra War of the 1980s.

Nearly thirty years after the revolution, there is still a strong Sandinista presence in politics, hundreds of well-meaning foreign volunteers still come to build schools and dig wells, and rural poverty is still a problem, but it would be wrong to see Nicaragua solely through the prism of its troubled past.

Great advances have been made in recent years to modernize and bring better education and health services to remote rural areas. The road network has been vastly improved, opening up isolated parts of the country. Perhaps the biggest recent change is that the traditional mainstays of the economy—beef, coffee, and gold—have now been joined by tourism, a generator of jobs that is also benefiting the naive artists of the Solentiname Islands, the potters of the Pueblos Blancos near Masaya, and the coffee growers, chocolate makers, tobacco brands, and rum makers who have earned an international reputation for the high quality of their wares.

To give a broader overview of the country this book has highlighted the vibrant folk traditions and *fiestas* that have been recognized by UNESCO, the rich tradition of poetry and literature represented by the maestro Rubén Darío and modern writers like Ernesto Cardenal, Gioconda Belli, and Sergio Ramírez, and the legendary fighters who have put Nicaragua on the map of great boxing nations.

In essence, the true magic of Nicaragua is that it continually serves up surprises. Whether you are a tourist, a business traveler, or an expat looking to relocate, we hope the careful research outlined in this overview will arm you with the insights and language tips that will make your trip more rewarding and give you a better understanding of how Nicaraguans live, how they love, and how they do business.

Further Reading

Belli, Gioconda. *The Country Under My Skin: A Memoir of Love and War*. New York: Anchor Books, 2003.

Cardenal, Ernesto. *Pluriverse: New and Selected Poems*. New York: New Directions, 2009.

Chavarria-Duriaux, Liliana; David C. Hille; Robert Dean. *Birds of Nicaragua*. Ithaca: Cornell University Press, 2018.

Dando-Collins, Stephen. T*ycoon's War: How Cornelius Vanderbilt Invaded a Country to Overthrow America's Most Famous Military Adventurer*. Boston: Da Capo Press, 2009.

Darío, Rubén. *Selected Writings*. London: Penguin Classics, 2005.

Feiling, Tom. *The Island That Disappeared: Old Providence and the Making of the Western World*. London: Explore Books, 2017.

Gage, Eleni N. *The Ladies of Managua*. New York: St Martin's Press, 2016.

Kinzer, Stephen. *Blood of Brothers: Life and War in Nicaragua*. Cambridge, MA: Harvard University Press, 2007.

Marriot, Edward. *Savage Shore: Life and Death with Nicaragua's Last Shark Hunters*. New York: Holt Paperbacks, 2001.

Martínez-Sanchez, Juan Carlos (et al). *A Guide to The Birds of Nicaragua*. Hohenwarsleben: Westarp Wissenschaften, 2014.

Ramírez, Sergio. *Adiós Muchachos: A Memoir of the Sandinista Revolution*. Duke University Press, 2011.

Ramírez, Sergio. *Margarita, How Beautiful the Sea*. Evanston, Illinois: Curbstone Books, 2007.

Rushdie, Salman. *The Jaguar Smile*. New York: Random House, 2008.

Walker, Thomas W. *Nicaragua: Emerging from the Shadow of the Eagle*. Boulder, Colorado: Westview Press, 2016.

Walker, William. *The War in Nicaragua*. University of Arizona Press, 1985.

Zimmerman, Mathilde. *Sandinista: Carlos Fonseca and the Nicaraguan Revolution*. Durham, North Carolina: Duke University Press, 2001.

culture smart! nicaragua

Index

Acknowledgments

I dedicate this book to Francisco de Jesus, my beloved son, and my parents Derek and Shirley Maddicks who have inspired and supported me on my often bumpy journey as a travel writer. I also owe a great debt of gratitude to Nicaraguan friends Elizabet Castillo, Mauricio Alberto López, and the people of San Francisco Libre, whose small town is twinned with my home town of Reading. The Nicaraguan ambassador to the UK, Guisell Morales, has been a huge support, as have

Nicaraguan Tourism Minister Anasha Campbell, all the staff at INTUR, and Jan Strik of Vapues Tours, whose love for his adopted home is infectious.